THE PRACTICAL GUIDE TO

PERSONAL SECURITY

Become a Competent and Confident Stakeholder in Your Own Safety

ROB CHADWICK

Former Head of the FBI's Tactical Training Program

FOREWORD BY WILLIAM P. BARR
Former United States Attorney General

ISBN: 979-8-218-68646-8
First Edition

Published by: Holdfast Security Group, LLC

Edited by: Books You Can Trust, LLC
Cover design and interior formatting by: Emily Silvernail

DISCLAIMER: This manual is for informational purposes only. The techniques and suggestions described herein are intended solely for educational use. By reading or applying any of the material, you voluntarily accept all responsibility and liability. The author, publisher, editor, and contributors disclaim all liability for any injury, loss, or damage resulting from the use or misuse of the information contained in this manual.

Printed in the United States of America

For all those who are seeking to live their lives free from the tyranny of fear—may this guide serve as a resource—empowering you to stand confident, live boldly, and embrace each day with peace of mind.

AUTHOR'S NOTE

Photo by Delta Defense LLC

The decision to write *The Practical Guide to Personal Security* was born from a simple but profound belief: that every person deserves to live free from the tyranny of fear. Too often, personal security is approached from a place of anxiety and helplessness. While the world certainly presents real dangers, living in constant fear is neither healthy nor necessary. True security isn't about building walls around your life—it's about building confidence within it.

This belief took root in me at a young age. Growing up, I spent a lot of time with my grandparents—both of whom lived life to the fullest. But when my grandfather passed away, it broke my heart to see how his passing left my grandmother feeling utterly vulnerable. She had lost not only her husband but also the person she had always seen as her protector. That loss of personal security seemed to rob her of the very joy of living.

Though she was a healthy, active woman with many good years ahead of her, she began living under a constant sense of dread, feeling helpless against the whims of a random criminal. She withdrew from the life she once embraced so fully. But then something remarkable happened. My

5

uncle, a police officer, bought her a firearm and took the time to help her become truly proficient with it. He made sure she understood not just how and when to use it, but also helped her develop a practical home security plan. With some basic upgrades around the house and a simple, effective plan to fall back on, I witnessed an incredible transformation.

My grandmother became a true stakeholder in her own safety and security. That sense of empowerment restored her confidence—and with it, her joy for living. She wasn't just surviving; she was thriving again. It was that example, more than anything else, that inspired me to dedicate my career to helping others live their lives free from the crippling anxiety caused by fear.

This book is a product of that mission. Inside, you'll find practical steps, proven strategies, and a mindset rooted in awareness, preparation, and personal empowerment. Whether you're looking to secure your home, navigate your community with greater confidence, travel safely, or better protect those you care about, this guide is here to help. But more importantly, it's here to remind you that fear should never be the thing that defines or limits your life.

Thank you for allowing me to walk this path with you.

Stay safe. Live free.

Rob Chadwick

Rob Chadwick

FBI Supervisory Special Agent (retired), 30 year law enforcement career, FBI Tactical Training Unit Chief, FBI Master Instructor, FBI Principle Firearms Instructor, FBI Principle Tactical Instructor, FBI Emergency Vehicle Operations Instructor, FBI Protective Operations Instructor, Mass Casualty Event Response Instructor, Active Shooter Response Senior Instructor, SWAT Tactical Medic, Emergency Medical Technician, TASER Master Instructor, 2017 International Keynote Speaker on Active Shooter Response in Prague (Czech Republic), Director of Education and Training at the U.S. Concealed Carry Association, Security Expert and Industry Consultant — Founder of Holdfast Securitiy Group, Former Police Office and K9 handler with the Fairfax County (Virginia) Police Department Special Operations Division

TABLE OF CONTENTS

FOREWORD

By William P. Barr
Former Attorney General of the United States

In an era defined by uncertainty and increasingly complex threats to our personal safety, the importance of preparedness and vigilance has never been greater. Security is no longer a concern reserved solely for governments and law enforcement agencies—it is a personal responsibility that every citizen must embrace. Whether in our homes, our workplaces, or the public spaces we frequent, the ability to recognize danger and respond decisively is a skill set vital to safeguarding our lives and the lives of those we hold dear.

The Practical Guide to Personal Security is far more than a handbook; it is a blueprint for living with confidence in an unpredictable world. It offers clear, actionable strategies grounded in real-world experience and sound judgment. This guide empowers individuals to take control of their personal safety with the same diligence and seriousness one would devote to securing their financial future or protecting their health.

I speak from experience when I say that the guidance offered within these pages is not theoretical—it is proven. As a 30-year law enforcement veteran, Rob ultimately led the tactical training program at Quantico for the FBI. During my tenure as Attorney General, he was a senior member of my personal security detail, serving with unwavering professionalism, sound judgment, and an unshakable commitment to duty. In the most sensitive environments, I relied upon his expertise. His calm demeanor under pressure and meticulous attention to every detail made all the difference in moments when vigilance was paramount.

Now, Rob has taken the lessons forged through years of dedicated service and distilled them into this indispensable guide. His experience is not drawn from abstract theory, but from standing on the front lines, facing real threats, and making critical decisions when lives were on the line.

The right to protect oneself is among our most fundamental liberties, but it comes with the solemn duty to do so responsibly and lawfully. This guide provides the tools and mindset necessary to uphold that duty with honor. Rooted in respect for the law, concern for our communities, and a steadfast commitment to preserving the safety and dignity of the innocent, this book is a critical resource for anyone serious about personal security.

Throughout my career in public service and law enforcement, I have seen firsthand the devastating consequences of complacency in the face of criminal threats. I have also seen the remarkable difference that preparation, awareness, and prudent action can make in moments of crisis. This book distills those hard-earned lessons into practical strategies that are accessible to all—whether you are a seasoned professional or someone taking their first steps toward a more secure life.

I commend Rob Chadwick for this vital contribution to the ongoing dialogue about self-reliance and safety. His insights are hard-earned and his advice, time-tested. May this work serve as both a guide and an inspiration to all who choose to live prepared and stand vigilant in an ever-changing world.

INTRODUCTION

*We sleep soundly in our beds, because rough men
stand ready in the night to visit violence upon
those who would do us harm.*

– George Orwell

For nearly a century, this sentiment—often attributed to figures like George Orwell or perhaps Winston Churchill—accurately described life in America. Whether acknowledged or not, Americans have long benefited from an era of unprecedented law enforcement excellence. The professionalism, experience, and technological advancements of police forces across the country provided a foundation of security that allowed most people to go about their daily lives without a second thought.

That era is over.

The security environment in the United States has shifted dramatically in recent years, and not for the better. The effects of the "Defund the Police" movement, combined with rising crime rates and a significant decline in law enforcement recruitment and retention, have created an urgent need for personal vigilance and preparedness.

The unfortunate reality is that law enforcement response times have skyrocketed, departments across the country are struggling to retain qualified officers, and the level of training many officers receive is far below what the public assumes. In many cases, police agencies are underfunded, overstretched, and unable to provide the level of security citizens once took for granted.

For those paying attention, this means one thing: *your personal security is now your personal responsibility.*

This book is designed to equip you with the knowledge, mindset, and practical skills to navigate today's security landscape. We will begin with a candid assessment of the current security environment, detailing how the backlash against law enforcement has led to real and lasting consequences for the average citizen.

We will examine what it means to face a critical situation, the realities of violent crime, and the importance of early detection and avoidance. From situational awareness to the physiological and psychological responses to a crisis, we will explore how to prepare for—and survive—a violent encounter.

While the topic of self-defense often sparks debate, the truth is that **in some situations, physical violence is the only answer** that will ensure your survival. Whether it's using non-lethal force, physical combatives, or firearms, we will discuss what it means to fight back and how to do so effectively. Beyond the physical confrontation, we will also address the legal, civil, and social ramifications of self-defense, as well as how to develop a personal security plan tailored to your home, workplace, and public life.

The goal of this book is not to instill fear, but to foster confidence. The world has changed, and while we may wish for the security of the past, we must adapt to the realities of today. With the right mindset, training, and preparation, you can take control of your own safety.

Our New Reality

The security environment in the United States has undergone a *fundamental and irreversible shift* in the wake of the "Defund the Police" movement, societal unrest, and widespread law enforcement staffing shortages.

This isn't speculation. I base this conclusion on firsthand experience. On May 25, 2020—the day George Floyd died—I was serving as the Chief of the FBI's Tactical Training Unit at Quantico, responsible for preparing Special Agents to face the worst-case scenarios of their profession.

My unit also trained our law enforcement partners across the country and internationally, conducting "Law Enforcement Training for Safety & Survival" (LETSS) courses—intensive, reality-based training programs designed to sharpen officers' tactical, firearms, and decision-making skills. This work provided me with an *unparalleled perspective* on the front lines of law enforcement across the United States.

What I saw after 2020 was stark.

The Unraveling of Law Enforcement

The "Defund" movement was a bell that cannot be unrung. The impact has been devastating—not just for police officers but for the citizens they serve.

Consider these realities:

- Law enforcement agencies across the country are struggling to recruit and retain officers. Where *hundreds* of candidates once competed for open positions, departments now struggle to find a *handful* of minimally qualified applicants.
- Academy classes are being canceled. There simply aren't enough recruits to justify running them.
- *Experienced officers* are leaving the profession in record numbers—retiring early or quitting altogether.
- Response times have doubled nationwide.[1] In an emergency, it now takes the police *twice as long* to arrive as it did just a few years ago.
- In the U.S., a home burglary, or break-in, occurs roughly every 26 seconds.[2]
- Many departments are operating below *minimum patrol staffing* levels at any given time, forcing agencies to prioritize staffing over training.

This last point is crucial. Training is what builds confidence, competence, and decisiveness in officers. Without it, hesitation increases. And in law enforcement, hesitation can be fatal.

The result? A vicious cycle:

1. **Officers hesitate**, unsure if their department or community will support them in a use-of-force incident.
2. That hesitation gets officers **hurt or killed**. From 2021 to 2023,

---

[1]Martin Kaste, "Why Data from 15 Cities Shows Police Response Times Are Taking Longer," Morning Edition, NPR, January 17, 2023, https://www.npr.org/2023/01/17/1149455678/why-data-from-15-cities-show-police-response-times-are-taking-longer.

[2]Federal Bureau of Investigation, Crime in the U.S. 2019: Crime Clock, accessed June 5, 2025, https://ucr.fbi.gov/crime-in-the-u.s/2019/crime-in-the-u.s.-2019/topic-pages/crime-clock.

more officers were feloniously killed than in any other consecutive three-year period in the past two decades.[3]
3. **Fewer people** want to join law enforcement, and more experienced officers choose to leave.
4. The remaining officers are stretched thin and **undertrained**, leading to longer response times and more hesitation.

Regardless of where you stand on policing, this affects you.

Every single one of us, at some point, will call 911 in a moment of crisis—praying that help arrives in time. But what if it doesn't?

You Are Your Own First Responder

The reality is clear: The security environment in the U.S. has changed, and it is unlikely to improve in the foreseeable future.

This new reality must be factored into your personal and family security planning. You can no longer afford to outsource your safety to the police. The responsibility for your protection—and the protection of your loved ones—**now rests with you.**

This book is designed to help you take charge of your personal security. It will provide you with the knowledge, mindset, and strategies to ensure that you are not just a passive bystander in your own safety, but an active and prepared participant.

How do you detect and *avoid threats* before they materialize?

How do you develop a *situational awareness* mindset that allows you to see danger before it sees you?

What are the *legal, moral, and practical* considerations of self-defense?

How do you create a *personal security plan* for your home, workplace, and public life?

---

[3]Federal Bureau of Investigation, Officers Killed and Assaulted in the Line of Duty, 2023 Special Report, and Law Enforcement Employee Counts, Crime Data Explorer, accessed June 3, 2025, https://cde.ucr.cjis.gov.

What can you do after a serious injury to *sustain life* until definitive help arrives? What do you do when the police arrive *after* a self-defense incident?

An informed decision is always a superior one. No matter who you are or where you live, your security plan must begin with the acceptance of a simple but profound truth:

You are your own first, best, and often <u>only</u> true line of defense.

This book will show you how to embrace that responsibility. Welcome to *The Practical Guide to Personal Security*. Your journey to becoming a **competent** and **confident** stakeholder in your own safety and security—and realizing the peace of mind that comes with that empowerment—starts now.

CHAPTER 1

Accepting Reality—It Could Happen to You

What is a Critical Situation?

A critical situation is any event that demands an immediate response to preserve life and prevent serious harm. These moments unfold in an instant, often without warning, and require decisive action. Whether it's an armed robbery, home invasion, or physical assault, a critical situation is defined by its unpredictability and the necessity for swift, effective decision-making.

A key characteristic of these incidents is **time compression**—there is no luxury of extended deliberation. Unlike controlled environments where we can assess options, weigh risks, and make informed choices, a critical situation forces you to act in the present moment, often within seconds.

The most dangerous assumption a person can make is believing they will never find themselves in such a scenario. Many who have experienced violent encounters had convinced themselves that they lived in a safe neighborhood, that crime happened "to other people," or that the police would always be there to help. Reality tells a different story.

The 7-Second Rule: The Brutal Speed of Violent Encounters

One of the most sobering truths about violent crime is that it happens **fast,** typically within *7 seconds* from beginning to end. This is not an arbitrary number; it's based on real-world data and the analysis of violent encounters across countless incidents.

Here's how a 7-second violent event unfolds:

> **Second 1:** The predator initiates action. This could be an ambush, a gun drawn, or a sudden physical attack.

Second 2: You react, but your brain is still catching up, processing what's happening.

Second 3-4: The physical engagement occurs. If you're caught off guard, this could be a deadly blow, a gunshot, or a rapid struggle for control.

Second 5-6: The outcome is largely determined. Either the attacker has achieved their objective, or the victim has managed to fight back and shift the dynamic.

Second 7: The event is over. Either you're safe, the attacker has fled, or the damage is done.

This window of time is so brief that traditional reliance on external protection (such as calling 911) is impractical. Your response in those first few seconds is the difference between survival and tragedy.

The question isn't "Will the police come?"—it's "Can I *survive* long enough for help to arrive?"

The Rise in Violent Crime and Soaring Homicide Rates

The United States is witnessing a disturbing rise in violent crime, particularly homicides, aggravated assaults, and carjackings. Since the onset of the "Defund the Police" movement, major cities have experienced an explosion in crime rates:

- **Homicides have increased by over 30% in many metropolitan areas** since 2020, with many major cities seeing record-breaking numbers of murders in recent years.[4]

- **Police response times have skyrocketed**, often taking 15 minutes or more in emergencies, long after a violent encounter has ended.[5]

- **Criminals have become more brazen**, emboldened by the erosion of law enforcement presence and the lack of prosecutorial consequences in some jurisdictions.

This is not fearmongering; this is statistical reality. While politicians and media outlets debate the causes, the facts remain: violent criminals are operating with greater impunity, and the burden of self-protection has shifted onto the individual.

The solution is not panic—it is preparedness. The purpose of this book is not to frighten you but to provide you with the tools and knowledge necessary to avoid, de-escalate, and, if necessary, *fight back* against violence.

Recognizing the Signs of Impending Violence

Violence is rarely as random as it seems. While some crimes are spontaneous, many criminals exhibit pre-attack indicators that a trained observer can recognize. These include:

- **Unusual proxemics:** A person closing the distance in an unnatural or rapid way.

- **Indexing gestures:** Fidgeting with clothing, repeatedly touching or adjusting the waistband (often where weapons are hidden). Remember—approximately 90% of the population is right-hand-

---

[4]Council on Criminal Justice, Homicide Trends Report, accessed June 9, 2025, https://counciloncj.org/homicide-trends-report/.

[5]Martin Kaste, "Why Data from 15 Cities Shows Police Response Times Are Taking Longer," Morning Edition, NPR, January 17, 2023, https://www.npr.org/2023/01/17/1149455678/why-data-from-15-cities-show-police-response-times-are-taking-longer.

ed—a firearm or other concealed weapon will often be secured on the right hip or appendix area.

- **Target glancing:** The suspect is scanning for exits or avenues of escape after the attack. This includes intentionally noting security cameras, witnesses, or bystanders who may try to intervene, or the presence of law enforcement just before engaging.

- **Verbal deception:** Attempts to distract you with a question or request while positioning for an attack.

Recognizing these signs, even a few seconds before an attack, can provide *precious time* to react, move, or prepare for action.

Mindset: The Foundation of Survival

The **difference between victims and survivors** is not physical ability—it is mindset. The single most common denominator among those who have achieved a positive outcome during a critical event is that they had devoted time and consideration *ahead of time* to what they would do "if".

Your ability to recognize a critical situation, react decisively, and overcome hesitation is the *single* most important factor in determining your survival.

- **Accept reality:** Crime is real, it can happen to you, and law enforcement is not likely to be there in time to save you. Acknowledging this truth is the first step toward being prepared.

- **Pre-made decisions:** Think about how you would react before you ever need to. Develop a plan and run mental rehearsals of what you would do in a violent encounter. Spend time developing these plans for those situations and environments that you most often find yourself in - at home, at work, or out in public. These "pre-made" decisions will allow you to act quickly and decisively, stealing back those precious seconds, gaining you that most precious of commodities during any crisis: time.

- **Refuse to be a victim:** A committed mindset is more valuable than any weapon. A determined response can turn the tables on an attacker.

Final Thoughts

A **critical situation** is not a theoretical construct—it is a reality that people face every day. Violent crime is rising, attacks are happening faster than most people realize, and the ability to respond within seconds is essential.

By understanding the dynamics of violent encounters, recognizing pre-attack indicators, and adopting a survival mindset, you drastically improve your chances of making it through an encounter alive.

CHAPTER 2

The Power of Intuition: Your Built-in Security Alarm

Your intuition is one of the most **powerful self-defense** tools you possess. Often dismissed as a "gut feeling," intuition is actually your brain *subconsciously* processing environmental anomalies before you *consciously* recognize them.

This is a critical point to remember and incorporate into your personal security planning: By definition, you will likely not be fully aware of what is causing your brain to signal potential trouble. I'm not advocating that you get up and run out of the room every time you get an "uneasy" feeling … but I am recommending that you acknowledge that something *may* be amiss and that you take a moment to investigate further.

Think of it as an **early warning system**—an alert that something is off before you can logically explain why. Your subconscious constantly scans for danger, drawing from past experiences, social cues, and sensory input. Unfortunately, many people ignore their intuition because they don't want to appear rude or overreact. **This is a mistake.**

How to Leverage Intuition for Safety

1. **Acknowledge It:** If something *feels wrong*, don't dismiss it. Your subconscious may have detected a genuine threat before your rational mind catches up.

2. **Assess the Situation:** Look around. What's triggering your discomfort? A person's behavior? The way a group is positioned? An unusual silence?

3. **Act Accordingly:** Don't wait for confirmation. Trusting intuition may mean **leaving an area, altering your route, or preparing to defend yourself.** If you later realize there was no actual danger, no harm was done. If there was a real threat, your quick action may have saved your life.

Example of Ignoring vs. Trusting Intuition

Ignoring: You're walking alone, and you notice someone *shadowing your movements*, but you convince yourself it's just a coincidence. Moments later, they close the distance and launch an attack.

Trusting: You sense something is off. In response, you **cross the street, enter a populated store, or prepare a defensive tool.** The predator sees this and disengages, looking for an easier target. Your "gut feeling" is there for a reason. *Listen to it.*

Understanding the Predator: How Criminals Think

Photo by Delta Defense, LLC

To protect yourself, you must **understand how criminals select their victims.** Most criminals are not looking for a fight—they are looking for an easy target.

Common Criminal Tactics

Target Selection: Criminals seek out victims who appear *distracted, unaware, or physically isolated* and vulnerable. They look for people absorbed in their phones, walking alone with headphones in, or carrying heavy items that hinder movement or limit awareness.

Testing Boundaries: Many predators probe their targets before attacking. This may include *getting too close*, asking seemingly harmless questions, or lightly touching you to gauge your reaction. If you don't set boundaries, they see you as a compliant, easy victim.

Deception and Manipulation: Criminals often *use charm, lies, or fake emergencies* to lure people into compromising situations. They may pretend to need help changing a tire, be "looking" for a lost pet, ask to borrow your phone after a supposed "accident", or even act as an authority figure to get you to comply.

Ambush Strategies: Many violent encounters *begin with an ambush*. A predator will use cover (cars, corners, doorways) to hide before striking. Others work in teams, with one person distracting you while another moves in from behind.

Your best defense? Recognizing these behaviors early and acting decisively to avoid them.

Exploiting Polite Society:
How Criminals Use Social Norms Against You

One of the biggest reasons people fail to act on their intuition is **social conditioning.** Society teaches us to be polite to avoid appearing rude or judgmental. Criminals know this, *and they exploit it.*

Ways Criminals Exploit Social Norms

Using Guilt: "Why won't you help me? Are you really that selfish?" They *pressure you* into compliance.

Feigning Helplessness: "I just need directions; can you take a minute and help me?" They use *fake vulnerability* to get close.

Playing on Sympathy: "My wallet was stolen and I don't have enough money for bus fare." They *rely on your good nature* to isolate you and get you to lower your defenses.

Breaking Free from "Politeness"

Your safety comes first. If something feels wrong, walk away. You don't need an excuse.

Set firm boundaries. If someone makes you uncomfortable, say "No" with confidence and do not engage further.

Don't let social pressure override safety. If an elevator door opens and someone inside makes you uneasy, wait for the next one. If a stranger asks for help in a secluded area, don't go—direct them to a public place instead.

Listen to discomfort, *not guilt*. If you feel uncomfortable, remove yourself from the situation.

Self-Empowerment: Taking Control of Your Safety

Photo by Delta Defense, LLC

Many people mistakenly believe law enforcement or security professionals are responsible for their safety. While police play a role, the first line of defense is YOU.

Empowerment in personal security means taking responsibility for your own well-being. This is not paranoia—it is preparation.

Steps to Self-Empowerment

Develop a safety mindset. Accept that your security is ultimately your responsibility. You are the only constant in your own safety equation.

Educate yourself. Learn about criminal tactics, situational awareness, and self-defense principles. Knowledge is power.

Train for readiness. Regularly practice situational awareness and consider taking a self-defense and/or weapons training course. Confidence comes from preparation.

Establish boundaries. Be assertive in saying NO, don't be afraid to stand up for yourself, and walk away from potential trouble.

Empowerment does not mean living in fear. It means being prepared, informed, and willing to take action—in your own best interest—when needed.

Final Thoughts

In a world filled with distractions, noise, and social conditioning, your intuition remains one of the few unfiltered tools you can rely on for real-time personal security. It doesn't require permission, technology, or special training. It simply *requires that you listen*—and act.

We often underestimate our subconscious mind, relegating "gut feelings" to superstition or coincidence. But as this chapter has shown, **intuition is not mystical, it's biological**. It's your brain doing its job faster than your conscious mind can keep up. When paired with awareness, preparation, and the confidence to break free from social norms that don't serve your safety, intuition becomes a powerful, life-preserving asset.

Predators thrive on hesitation. They exploit politeness, manipulate sympathy, and count on you second-guessing yourself. But when you learn to honor that inner signal, you tip the scales in your favor. You become harder to surprise, less likely to freeze, and more likely to *take meaningful action early.*

Personal security isn't just about tools and tactics—it's about mindset. Intuition is your inner compass. It doesn't always shout; sometimes it just whispers. But in those whispers may lie the only warning you'll get.

So trust yourself. Listen closely. And when something doesn't feel right, don't explain it away—act.

Your safety is worth that moment of pause; it's worth being "rude," and it's certainly worth surviving to tell the story.

CHAPTER 3

The Best Defense:
Early Detection and Avoidance

The best fight is the one you never have to be in. While self-defense skills, weapons proficiency, and physical conditioning are valuable, they are secondary to the ability to detect and avoid threats before they escalate.

The safest and most effective way to protect yourself is to ensure that a confrontation never happens in the first place.

Avoidance is not cowardice—it's *strategy*.

Early detection allows you to recognize threats before they become active dangers. Whether you're walking through a parking garage, standing in line at a gas station, or navigating a crowded urban environment, staying alert and recognizing pre-attack indicators can prevent you from becoming a target.

Criminals and predators look for easy victims, those who appear distracted, unaware, or unprepared. The more you project confidence and awareness, the less appealing you become as a target.

Early Detection Saves Lives

By practicing situational awareness and threat recognition, you give yourself precious seconds to act. Those few seconds can be the difference between escaping unharmed and becoming a victim.

Simple Rules to Live By:

If you sense trouble, don't ignore it. Your subconscious mind often detects danger *before* your rational mind processes it. If something feels "off," trust your gut and take immediate action.

If someone tries to manipulate you, disengage. Many criminals use deception, guilt, or sympathy to lower your defenses. Don't allow politeness or social conditioning to override your safety instincts. If someone is invading your personal space, making you uncomfortable, or pushing your boundaries, *remove yourself* from the situation immediately.

If a situation feels wrong, remove yourself. Whether it's an escalating argument, an aggressive-looking crowd, or an unfamiliar person approaching too quickly, your safest option is almost always to leave. **You do not need to justify your actions to anyone.** Prioritize your safety over social norms.

Real-World Example:
How Early Detection Prevents Attacks

Imagine you're walking to your car in an empty parking garage. You notice a man seemingly loitering near your vehicle. Your intuition sends a warning—something about the situation feels wrong.

What are your options?

Ignore the warning and keep walking to your car.
This is the worst choice—you have no plan if he turns out to be a threat.

Stop and reassess.
Good choice—evaluate the man's behavior, check your surroundings, and determine if you are being followed.

Call someone while keeping your distance.
Great choice—predators prefer isolated victims.

Turn around and walk back to a safer location.
Best choice—you are not obligated to continue toward your vehicle. You can wait for the person to leave or find security to escort you.

By listening to intuition and recognizing potential danger early, you avoid a potential ambush scenario and stay in control of your safety.

Be Proactive, Not Reactive

The first step to survival is early detection. The second step is action.

- Stay aware of your surroundings.
- Trust your intuition and don't dismiss warning signs.
- Prioritize your safety over politeness or embarrassment.
- Act early to avoid being caught in a dangerous situation.

Avoidance is not weakness—it's the highest level of personal security. By detecting threats early and taking decisive action, you *dramatically* reduce your risk of becoming a victim. Situational awareness isn't just about seeing danger, it's about acting to ensure your safety.

Take Control of Your Personal Security

- Listen to your *intuition*, it's your early warning system.
- Understand how criminals operate to avoid their traps.
- *Break free* from politeness; your safety is more important than social norms.
- Empower yourself, your safety is your responsibility.
- Make *pre-made decisions* so you can act quickly under stress.
- Early detection and avoidance are the ultimate self-defense strategies.

By developing *situational awareness and self-empowerment*, you take control of your security—ensuring that you and your loved ones stay safe in an unpredictable world.

The Importance of Early Detection and Avoidance

Early detection of a threat provides *time to react* and escape. Avoiding a confrontation is always the best option when possible.

How to Enhance Early Detection:

- **Maintain 360-Degree Awareness:** Regularly scan your surroundings. Minimize distractions (such as cell phones) in non-secure spaces.

- **Identify Exits:** Always know where your escape routes are. Identity secondary (e.g., back door) and tertiary (e.g., window) routes,
if possible.

- **Recognize Anomalies:** If something seems out of place, pause. Remember your brain's bias towards normalcy!

- **Increase Vigilance in Transitional Spaces:** Parking lots, stairwells, and other isolated areas are common locations for attacks. Keep your head up, eyes and ears open, and free from distractions.

Heuristics: Time to Decide vs. Time to Act

Heuristic decision-making enables individuals to make rapid, effective decisions in high-stress or uncertain situations. In personal security, time is often a critical factor, and relying on heuristics—**mental shortcuts based on experience and instinct**—can mean the difference between safety and danger.

While analytical decision-making may be ideal in controlled environments, real-world security threats often require quick judgments based on limited information.

In a critical situation, you may be called upon to make a split-second, *life-or-death* decision that would take a room full of lawyers weeks to decide. Heuristic decision-making allows individuals to recognize patterns, assess risks, and act decisively *without* becoming paralyzed by over-analysis, making heuristics an essential tool for personal security preparedness.

Final Thoughts

By understanding intuition, recognizing criminal behaviors, and overcoming social conditioning, you can significantly improve your ability to detect and avoid danger.

Personal security is a **proactive effort** that requires awareness, preparation, the willingness to trust your instincts, and perhaps most importantly—*the willingness to act*—even when others don't or won't. The discipline to make and act upon pre-made decisions can mean the difference between safety and victimization.

Be alert, be empowered, and take control of your own security.

In the next chapter, we'll explore the foundational concept of **situational awareness,** the skill that allows you to detect threats early and avoid danger before it ever materializes.

CHAPTER 4

Situational Awareness: The Foundation of Personal Security

"Situational awareness" is often referenced but rarely well-defined. Many people mistakenly believe that simply "paying attention to your surroundings" is enough. While attentiveness is important, true situational awareness is a *deliberate and proactive* process that enables you to detect threats early, avoid danger, and react effectively when necessary.

Situational awareness is the ability to **perceive, understand, and anticipate** potential threats in your environment. It involves consciously assessing your surroundings, recognizing potential dangers, and taking proactive steps to avoid them. Situational awareness is not paranoia—it is the practice of staying alert and engaged in your surroundings to enhance your personal security.

Situational awareness is the cornerstone of personal security. Without it, no weapon, self-defense skill, or emergency plan will be effective—because if you fail to *recognize* a threat in time, you won't have the opportunity to act.

Situational Awareness:
Seeing the Danger vs. Taking Action

Many people misunderstand situational awareness as simply noticing what's happening around them. However, true situational awareness requires action.

- Noticing a suspicious person watching you is *awareness*.
- Crossing the street, changing your path, or entering a store to avoid them is *action*.
- Recognizing a group of people behaving aggressively in a bar is *awareness*.
- Leaving the bar before a fight breaks out is *action*.

Avoidance is Your Greatest Weapon

Every moment you delay action reduces your options. The sooner you detect a potential threat, the more choices you have:

- **Leave** before the situation escalates.
- Create **distance** between yourself and a potential threat.
- Mentally **prepare** to defend yourself if necessary.
- Call for assistance or **alert** others to the situation.

Fights, attacks, and violent encounters happen in seconds. If you only react when violence is unfolding, you're already way behind the curve. Early detection buys you time—and time gives you options.

Time is the single most crucial factor in any critical situation. Regardless of your physical fitness, self-defense skills, or weapons proficiency, none of it matters if you're caught off guard.

Professional protectors, such as executive security teams, operate under a guiding principle: **If a confrontation occurs, the mission has already failed.** Despite Hollywood's portrayal of bodyguards engaging in gunfights, real protection teams prioritize early detection and avoidance over confrontation.

For personal security, the same rule applies: Your goal is to *recognize and avoid* potential threats before they materialize. The following principles form the foundation of effective situational awareness.

The Building Blocks of Situational Awareness

1. Intentional Observation

True awareness begins with actively observing your environment. This means going beyond passive awareness and *deliberately engaging* with your surroundings:

- **Notice details** about people, objects, and behavior around you.
- **Mentally process** what you see—ask yourself, "Does anything look out of place?"
- **Adjust your awareness** level based on your environment (e.g., heightened vigilance in an unfamiliar or high-crime area).

While at home, security measures like reinforced doors, alarms, and window laminates can provide a **buffer zone**, allowing you to let your guard down when appropriate. In contrast, when you are in public spaces, you must remain alert.

Tip: When staying in a hotel, consider using a **security door wedge** to prevent unauthorized entry. Also, utilizing a portable door alarm or leaning a **folding ironing board** behind the door can serve to alert you if someone tries to enter while you sleep.

2. Minimize Distractions

The biggest enemy of situational awareness is distraction, especially smartphones and headphones.

- **Smartphones** destroy peripheral vision, especially at night.
- Noise-canceling **headphones** block crucial auditory cues, such as approaching footsteps or verbal warnings.
- **Texting or scrolling** social media makes you an easy target for criminals looking for distracted victims.

Solution: Check your phone in a safe, controlled environment.

Do not use it while walking or waiting in public spaces. This rule applies in your car as well. You are extremely vulnerable just after getting into your car. If you need to enter an address into your navigation app, wait until you've driven a block or two away to do so. You can probably make it to the end of the street without Google Maps!

3. Stay Informed

Awareness isn't just about what's happening immediately around you—it's also about being informed of *developing* threats.

- **Know the crime trends** in the areas you frequent.
- **Enable emergency alerts** for local news and law enforcement updates.
- **Pay attention to public behavior**, crowd movements can signal danger before you see it directly.

Example: If you hear shouting or see people running in one direction, don't wait to investigate. *Leave the area immediately.*

4. Know Your Environment

Whenever you enter a new environment, **quickly scan** for exits, cover, and escape routes:

- Primary exit – The way you entered is often the most obvious escape route.

- Secondary exit – Look for fire exits, employee-only doors, or windows you can use in an emergency.
- Cover vs. Concealment – Cover stops bullets (concrete walls, parts of a car), while concealment only hides you (bushes, curtains). Concealment is better than nothing, cover is better than concealment.

If a violent situation erupts, having a pre-planned escape strategy can *save your life.*

5. Maintain a Broad Perspective

One of the biggest threats to situational awareness is **tunnel vision**—focusing too much on a single detail while ignoring the bigger picture.

Example: A stranger asks for the time, but instead of only focusing on them, *scan your surroundings.* Is someone else approaching from another angle? Is there a potential ambush scenario forming?

Criminals often *work in teams* and use distractions to get close. Maintaining distance and peripheral awareness prevents you from being caught off guard.

6. Use All of Your Senses

Your intuition is your body's built-in early warning system. If something feels "off," don't ignore it.

- **Sight** – Look for suspicious behaviors, not just appearances.
- **Hearing** – Sudden silence in a normally loud area could indicate a threat.
- **Smell** – Unusual chemical or smoke odors might indicate a fire or hazard.
- **Touch** – If someone bumps into you unexpectedly, check your belongings immediately.

Example: If the hairs on the back of your neck stand up, trust that feeling and pay attention. It may be your subconscious detecting something unusual before your conscious mind processes it.

7. Assess People's Behavior

Human behavior can provide early warning signs of a threat. Some red flags include:

- **Fidgeting with clothing** – Could indicate a concealed weapon.
- **Constant scanning of the area** – Could mean that the person is looking for security or a getaway route.
- **Invasion of personal space** – Criminals will often try to get within arm's reach before launching an attack.

A calm but assertive posture and maintaining distance can deter potential attackers.

8. Identify Patterns and Anomalies

People are creatures of habit. When something deviates from the norm, it stands out—and should be evaluated as a potential threat.

Examples:

- You notice someone following you for several blocks, **stopping when you stop.**
- A person in a long coat enters a store on a hot day, glances around, but **doesn't shop**.
- A stranger **changes direction** to intersect your path multiple times.

Recognizing these anomalies *gives you time* to take preemptive action—such as changing direction, seeking a crowded area, or preparing a defensive tool.

9. Anticipate Changes and Be Prepared to Act

Situations can escalate *rapidly*. If you see tensions rising, protests forming, or sudden chaos, **leave immediately**—before it turns violent.

Example: An incident caught on surveillance camera showed an argument between two groups inside a crowded shopping mall food court area. Many innocent bystanders became aware of the disturbance as the argument became more heated. Sensing trouble, only one table of diners got up and quickly left the area *just seconds* before one of the individuals involved in the argument pulled out a gun and began shooting.

Despite observing what was a rapidly escalating argument between two groups of strangers, most of the bystanders **failed to leave** the area. Instead, they were caught up in the spectacle of this argument that had nothing to do with them.

Only those few people who had recognized the developing trouble and took action to move away were safely around a corner when the bullets began to fly. Situational awareness and a moment of early action, leaving when they recognized the potential for violence, allowed them to put **time and distance** between themselves and a potentially deadly situation.

10. Stay Calm and Take Decisive Action

In a crisis, hesitation *can be fatal.* A common denominator among many people who have survived violent situations is that they had devoted time and consideration—ahead of time—to what they would do "if." They had developed **pre-made decisions** about what they would do in a given situation and committed themselves to *act* on those decisions.

- **Understand and Anticipate the "Normalcy Bias"** – Your brain will try to rationalize anomalies (e.g., gunfire as fireworks or a car backfiring), and you may begin to internally deny what is unfolding: "This can't be happening."
- **Commit to action** – Even if others are reluctant to move, those few seconds that you gain in a crisis may make all the difference.
- **Trust your plan** – If you have rehearsed responses (e.g., where to take cover, how to escape), you'll act instinctively rather than panic and risk being overcome by events.

Situational awareness is the cornerstone of personal security, requiring a **proactive** mindset and deliberate observation of your surroundings. It isn't a single skill—it's *a mindset*.

It's about committing to **active** observation, minimizing distractions, and thinking one step ahead. By integrating these building blocks into your daily life, you're not just reacting to the world around you, you're taking control of your personal safety.

The goal is not to live in fear, but to live **prepared**: calm, observant, and ready to act with clarity when it counts.

Barriers to Situational Awareness

- **Distractions:** Smartphones, social media, and entertainment can divert attention from immediate surroundings.

- **Complacency:** Assuming that danger is unlikely can lead to a false sense of security.

- **Cognitive Overload:** Stress, exhaustion, and multitasking can reduce the ability to notice potential threats.

- **Lack of Training:** Many people have never been taught to assess their surroundings for threats or recognize the behavior of a potential predator.

- **Over-reliance on Authority:** Some individuals assume that law enforcement or security personnel will handle all threats, leading to personal inaction.

Incorporating Situational Awareness Into Daily Life

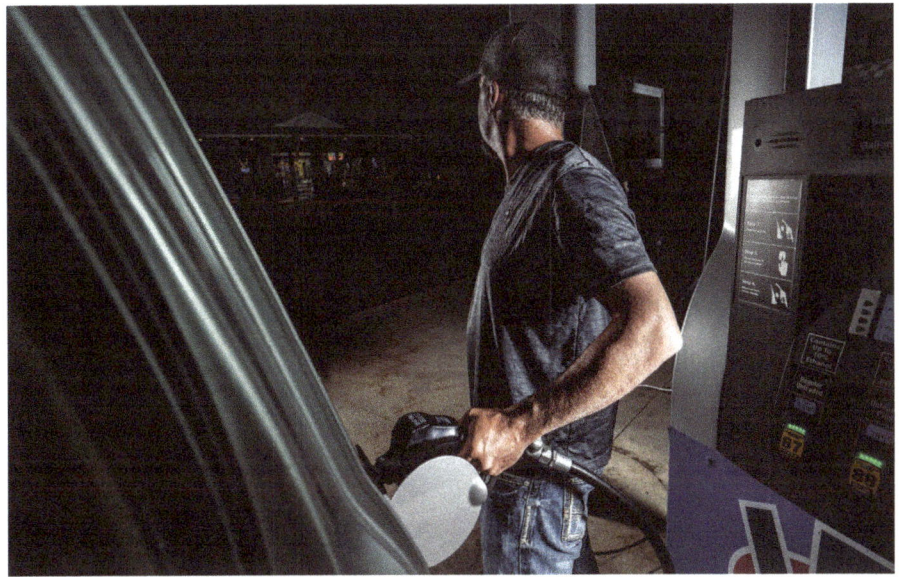

Photo by Delta Defense, LLC

Situational awareness is not paranoia—it is a proactive mindset that enhances safety while allowing you to move through the world with confidence.

- **Train** your brain to notice details and patterns.
- **Minimize** distractions and stay engaged with your surroundings.
- **Trust** your intuition and empower yourself to act.

By incorporating these principles into daily life, you develop a **self-reliant security mindset**, ensuring that you and your loved ones remain a hard target in an unpredictable world.

"Pre-Made" Decisions: The Power of Planning

One of the most effective ways to respond to threats is to develop what I call "pre-made decisions". These are **pre-determined actions** to take in a crisis. Making critical, split-second decisions under extreme stress is difficult at best, but having a well-thought-out plan—in advance—significantly increases the chances of a successful outcome.

In a critical moment, you will not have time for *nor be capable of complex decision-making*. Acute stress related to a sudden, existential threat significantly narrows your field of vision, almost completely occludes your hearing, and slows thought processing.

In a moment of extreme peril, hesitation can be deadly. Pre-made decisions help to mitigate hesitation in an emergency.

Understanding Pre-Made Decisions

Pre-made decisions allow us to determine—before a crisis happens—when and how to respond to a sudden threat. This saves valuable time and enables us to act decisively during the critical moments of a dangerous situation. To illustrate this concept, I often use what I call the:

"Gas Station Robbery Scenario"

Imagine I've ignored my own advice about when and where to refuel my car and find myself forced to stop for gas in a high-crime area late at night with few people around.

As I stand at the pump, distracted while fueling, an armed individual wielding a weapon approaches and demands, "Give me your keys and wallet, or I'll kill you."

Legally speaking, this situation would likely justify the use of force, including lethal force, in self-defense.* This individual has threatened serious bodily harm or even death if I don't comply with their demands. Almost everyone would agree that this meets the textbook definition of armed robbery, meaning **I would have legal grounds to defend myself.**

Understanding the laws governing the use of force in your area is essential before making any self-defense decisions.

Now, as the Director of Training for the United States Concealed Carry Association, a 30-year law enforcement veteran, a long-time SWAT Operator, and former Principal Tactical Instructor for the FBI, I am almost always legally armed and am highly trained to respond to such situations. However, *my* pre-made decision in this scenario *may surprise you.*

Without hesitation, **I would throw my wallet in one direction and my car**

keys in another. As soon as the assailant moved to retrieve either, I would run *away* as fast as possible.

Why Would I Choose to Flee?

At first, this decision may seem unexpected, but it becomes clear when considering the potential consequences of a use-of-force incident. Even if I am justified in defending myself, the aftermath of such an event could be life-altering. At a minimum, I would likely face months—if not years—of **legal battles** to defend myself from potential criminal prosecution. The financial, emotional, and social toll on my family would be enormous—legal fees, lost work, damaged friendships, and even the possibility of incarceration.

This doesn't even take into account **civil lawsuits**, which often have a much lower burden of proof than criminal trials. The assailant (or their family) could sue me, as could bystanders who claim they were traumatized by witnessing the event. Even if I were found innocent, the legal process would be devastating financially and emotionally.

With all of this in mind, my pre-made decision is simple: my car is insured, and everything inside it is replaceable. My wallet holds cancelable credit cards and little cash. Within a few days, I could replace my car, my driver's license, and my credit cards, which would be **an inconvenience, but not a life-altering event.**

When the Calculation Changes

Now, let's slightly alter this scenario. Suppose everything remains the same, except my 18-month-old grandson is strapped into his car seat inside the vehicle. Would that change my decision? *Absolutely.*

In this case, I wouldn't hesitate to use whatever force was necessary to ensure my grandson's safety. The risks—legal, financial, and personal—become irrelevant when compared to the safety of my loved one. Like any parent or grandparent, *I've already made this calculation.* My pre-made decision in this scenario is clear: I will do whatever it takes to make sure that child goes home safely.

Having these decisions already made allows me to react with **greater speed,**

clarity, and confidence, dramatically improving my chances of survival and success in a life-threatening situation.

Final Thoughts

Situational awareness is more than just a skill—it is a mindset, a way of operating in the world that keeps you ahead of potential threats. The ability to perceive, assess, and act **before** danger unfolds is the foundation of personal security. Without it, even the best self-defense training or tools will be ineffective.

By cultivating intentional observation, minimizing distractions, staying informed, and anticipating potential dangers, you equip yourself with the most powerful weapon of all: **time.** Time to recognize a threat before it materializes. Time to create distance. Time to avoid unnecessary confrontations.

Ultimately, true security is not about reacting to violence—it's about avoiding it entirely whenever possible. Professionals in the field of protection operate under the principle that if a confrontation occurs, the mission has *already* failed. This same philosophy applies to personal safety. The goal is not to win a fight but to **never be in one.**

By integrating situational awareness into your daily life, developing pre-made decisions, and understanding the importance of early detection and avoidance, you empower yourself to take control of your safety. Whether through recognizing behavioral red flags, adjusting your level of alertness based on your environment, or deciding *in advance* how you will respond to a crisis, these principles allow you to move through life with confidence, security, and control.

Situational awareness is not paranoia—it is preparation. The more you train yourself to recognize danger before it strikes, the greater your ability to protect yourself and those you love. Stay aware. Stay prepared. Stay safe.

CHAPTER 5

Understanding Physiological, Psychological, & Sociological Responses During a Crisis

The Mind and Body Under Stress: What to Expect

When faced with a critical situation, the human body and mind undergo profound changes. These responses are evolutionary survival mechanisms designed to enhance our chances of survival. However, if unprepared, they can, *and will*, hinder effective decision-making and action. It is *critical* that you understand, anticipate, and incorporate strategies to mitigate these reactions when developing your personal security plans.

Physiological Responses to Crisis:

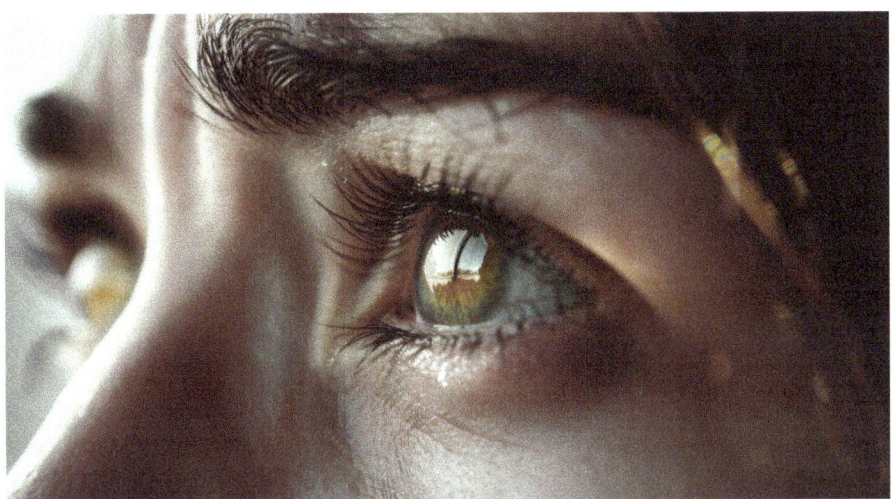

Adrenaline Surge (Fight, Flight, or Freeze Response)

- Increased heart rate and blood pressure
- Heightened senses

- Increased muscle tension and strength
- Faster breathing to oxygenate muscles

Cognitive Impairments

- Tunnel vision (focus narrows to the immediate threat, ignoring the surroundings)
- Auditory exclusion (loss of peripheral sounds)
- Impaired fine motor skills (shaky hands, difficulty manipulating objects like a key, firearm, can of pepper spray, or a phone)
- Time distortion (events seem to move in slow motion or, in some cases, too quickly)

Emotional Overload

- Panic, denial, hesitation, or paralysis due to fear
- Dissociation or detachment (feeling disconnected from reality)

Sociological Pressures:
How Society Conditions Us to Respond

Beyond the body's automatic responses, society imposes expectations that can affect how individuals react in a crisis. These pressures can either help or hinder survival.

Common Sociological Factors:

- **Fear of Overreaction:** Many hesitate to act because they worry about embarrassment, legal repercussions, or being seen as paranoid.

- **The Bystander Effect:** In public settings, people often *wait for others* to act first, assuming someone else will intervene.

- **Obedience to Authority:** Individuals may delay action if they believe they must wait for *permission* from an authority figure.

- **Social Conditioning Toward Compliance:** People are often conditioned to be **polite**, making them hesitant to resist forcefully.

How to Mitigate the Effects of Physiological and Sociological Pressures

Understanding and anticipating these reactions and training to overcome them can drastically improve survival chances in critical situations.

1. Combatting the Physiological Freeze

- **Controlled Breathing (Tactical Breathing):** Slow, deep breaths (4-second inhale, 4-second hold, 4-second exhale) help to regulate heart rate and clear the mind.

- **Mental Rehearsal:** Visualizing possible scenarios and responses can prepare the mind to act under stress. Remember: *the body cannot go where the mind has not already been.*

- **Physical Conditioning:** Regular exercise improves stamina and resilience to stress.

- **Desensitization Training:** Exposure to stress in controlled environments (e.g., self-defense classes, firearms training, scenario-based drills) conditions the body to function under pressure.

2. Overcoming Sociological Hesitation

- **Permission to Act:** *Give yourself permission right now* to take decisive action when necessary. You do not need to justify your instincts.

- **Breaking the Bystander Effect:** Commit to being the one who acts when danger arises. You will certainly increase your odds of achieving a positive outcome; you may very well influence others to take action as well.

- **Assertiveness Training:** Practice saying "No" firmly and enforcing personal boundaries without apology.

- **Awareness of Manipulation Tactics:** Recognizing social pressures and manipulation strategies can help you resist being coerced into inaction.

The Importance of a Commitment to Action

Many violent encounters are lost in the first few seconds due to hesitation. The most important factor in survival is the willingness to **act immediately** when a threat is identified.

Key Aspects of Committing to Action:

1. **Decisiveness:** The faster you respond, the greater your chances of survival.

2. **Training for Response:** Regular training builds "muscle memory," making it easier to act under stress.

3. **Pre-made Decisions:** Knowing in advance how you will react removes hesitation and allows you to "fall back" on a plan in critical moments.

4. **Accepting Reality:** Acknowledge that violence is sometimes unavoidable and commit to acting when necessary.

Final Thoughts

Understanding both physiological and sociological responses to crisis situations is essential to personal security. The body's automatic reactions can be managed with training, while societal pressures to comply or hesitate must be actively resisted. By conditioning yourself to take decisive action, you increase your ability to survive and protect yourself and those around you.

The key to personal security is not just awareness—it is **the ability and commitment to *act* when it matters most.**

CHAPTER 6

De-Escalation: Preventing Conflict Before It Starts

Personal security isn't just about physical defenses or tactical responses—it's also about mastering the social and psychological tools that can prevent a situation from escalating in the first place.

De-escalation is the process of calming a tense or potentially violent encounter before it becomes dangerous. This chapter explores the key principles, tactics, and mindset necessary for effective de-escalation.

Understanding the Psychology of Conflict

Conflict often arises from a perceived threat to one's identity, safety, or dignity. When people feel cornered, disrespected, or misunderstood, they may lash out in anger or defensiveness.

Understanding this core concept is the first step in mastering de-escalation. It's important to remember that de-escalation is not a sign of timidity—it's a manifestation of wisdom.

As a law enforcement officer, I employed de-escalation techniques far more frequently than combatives or firearms to resolve a conflict. Recognizing the key emotional drivers in a conflict —understanding where another person's reaction may be coming from—is critical in successfully de-escalating a potentially volatile situation:

Key emotional drivers include:

- **Fear:** Of harm, loss of control, or humiliation
- **Anger:** Often a mask for deeper feelings of vulnerability
- **Pride:** Especially when someone feels disrespected or challenged

The De-Escalator's Mindset

Approach every encounter with the goal of *resolution*, not *victory*. A calm, confident, and non-threatening presence is your greatest asset.

Principles to internalize:

- **Empathy:** Seek to understand the other person's perspective.
- **Patience:** Give the person time to express themselves.
- **Composure:** Control your own emotional state.
- **Non-judgment:** Avoid assumptions or blame.

Verbal Techniques

1. **Calm Tone & Volume:** Speak slowly, clearly, and at a lower volume to set a non-confrontational tone.

2. **Open-Ended Questions:** Encourage dialogue. For example, "Can you tell me what's going on?"

3. **Acknowledge Emotions:** Validate feelings without agreeing with hostile behavior. "I can see you're upset."

4. **Reflective Listening:** Repeat back what you hear to show understanding and build rapport.

5. **Set Boundaries:** Be clear and respectful when articulating what

is and isn't acceptable.

Non-Verbal Communication

- **Open Body Language:** Avoid crossing arms or clenching fists.
- **Neutral Facial Expression:** Show attentiveness without sarcasm or smirking.
- **Maintain Personal Space:** Avoid making the other person feel trapped or crowded.
- **Controlled Movements:** Sudden gestures can be misinterpreted.

Situational Strategies

- **Exit Strategy:** Always have a way to leave the situation quickly and safely.
- **Environmental Awareness:** Position yourself to observe escape routes and avoid being cornered.
- **Avoid Triggers:** Steer away from hot-button topics or accusatory language.
- **Enlist Allies:** If possible, involve calm third parties who can help defuse tension.

Real-World Examples:

Example 1: Verbal Aggression in a Parking Lot

You're walking back to your car in a busy lot when another driver accuses you of stealing their parking spot. They approach angrily, yelling and gesturing aggressively.

Instead of matching their energy or arguing, you calmly hold up your hand in a non-threatening way and say, "I didn't realize that spot was yours—I can move if you need it." You keep your tone even and sincere. After a pause, the driver exhales, waves you off, and walks away. You've just prevented a potential escalation with calm words and posture, and can go about the rest of your day.

Example 2: Argument at a Family Gathering

At a family barbecue, you notice two relatives beginning to argue heatedly about politics. Voices start to rise, and the conversation becomes tense. You gently interject, saying, "I know this is something you both care about, but maybe we can save this discussion for later. Let's grab some dessert and get back to enjoying the afternoon."

By redirecting the conversation without taking sides, you successfully help cool things off and preserve the peace.

When De-Escalation Fails

Despite your best efforts, some individuals may not respond to de-escalation. Know when to disengage.

- **Safety First:** If someone becomes violent or threatens harm, prioritize escape or defense.
- **Call for Help:** Law enforcement or trained professionals may be required.
- **Document the Incident:** For legal and safety reasons, make a record of what occurred.

Final Thoughts

De-escalation is a crucial, humane skill that can protect you and others from unnecessary conflict. It requires awareness, self-control, and a willingness to defuse rather than dominate. As part of your overall personal security strategy, these skills can be as vital as any lock, alarm, or self-defense technique.

Always remember that *your safety* is the top priority. The most effective de-escalation may sometimes be avoidance—choosing not to engage, removing yourself from a volatile environment, or walking away before things intensify. Trust your instincts. If a situation feels wrong, it probably is.

Avoiding confrontation altogether is not cowardice, *it's wisdom.* It takes strength to choose peace and protect yourself through non-engagement when appropriate.

In the end, the goal isn't to win an argument or assert dominance—it's to stay safe, maintain control, and preserve your well-being and that of others. De-escalation is not a weakness; it's a practical, *powerful* tool in your personal security toolkit.

CHAPTER 7

When Violence Is Unavoidable

While avoidance and de-escalation are *always* the preferred options in any dangerous situation, there are times when confrontation is unavoidable. When faced with imminent physical harm, violence may be the only effective response. Understanding *when* and *how* to use force can mean the difference between survival and victimization.

When Is Violence Justified?

- When faced with an immediate threat to life or serious bodily harm, to yourself or others.
- When escape is not an option and/or de-escalation has failed.
- When preemptive action is necessary to prevent a clear and *imminent* danger of death or serious bodily harm.

Self-Defense Options: Non-Lethal and Physical Combatives

Photo by Delta Defense, LLC

Not all self-defense situations require lethal force, and there are many "non-permissive" environments where a firearm is illegal to possess. Non-lethal options can be highly effective in incapacitating or neutralizing a threat while allowing for escape.

Non-Lethal Self-Defense Tools

- **Pepper Spray:** Can cause temporary blindness, intense pain, and respiratory distress, allowing time to escape.
- **TASERs & Stun Guns:** Can immobilize or dissuade an attacker temporarily, though effectiveness varies based on proximity and clothing.
- **Impact Weapons (Batons, Improvised Weapons):** Blunt force can incapacitate an attacker without being lethal.
- **Personal Alarms:** Loud alarms can deter attackers and alert bystanders to an emergency.

Physical Combatives

When forced into close-quarters combat, knowing basic self-defense techniques can provide a crucial advantage.

- **Targeting Weak Points:** Eyes, throat, groin, knees, and joints are high-value targets that can disable an attacker.
- **Striking Techniques:** Simple, high-percentage techniques like palm strikes, elbow strikes, and knee strikes can be effective in close combat—if delivered with sufficient force.
- **Escaping Grabs and Holds:** Learning how to break free from wrist grabs, chokeholds, and bear hugs can prevent an attacker from gaining control.
- **Ground Fighting:** Knowing how to fight from the ground is essential if taken down during an attack.

Lethal Self-Defense: Firearms and Their Role

Photo by Delta Defense, LLC

In situations where lethal force is the only option, firearms can provide the ultimate means of defense. There is a very good reason why most combative sports have graduated "belts" and/or weight classes. Size, strength, and speed almost always decide the outcome of a physical contest.

The firearm is the *one tool* that can come closest to **leveling the playing field** between two otherwise mismatched opponents. A famous ad campaign from the early days of repeating firearms sums this up well: "God created men … Colonel Colt made them equal."

One of the many wise blessings our forefathers bestowed upon Americans is our constitutionally guaranteed right to bear arms. However, simply owning a gun does nothing to increase your personal security. *Responsible and effective* firearm use requires regular training, practice, and an understanding of legal and moral implications.

The Reality of Firearm Defense

- **Firearms Are a Tool, Not a Guarantee:** Simply owning a gun does not ensure safety. Proficiency and confidence in use, maintenance, and mindset are critical.

- **Laws Vary by Jurisdiction:** Understanding self-defense laws, concealed carry regulations, and use-of-force policies is essential. Ignorance of the law is *never* a valid defense in court.

- **Training Is Non-Negotiable:** Regular practice at the range, "dry firing" and weapons manipulation, scenario-based training, and stress drills all improve effectiveness in real encounters.

- **Situational Awareness Is Key:** A firearm is only useful if you recognize a threat *before* it's too late.

When to Use Lethal Force

1. When an assailant poses an *imminent threat* of death or serious bodily harm to yourself or others.

2. When in your home and faced with a violent intrusion (depending on your local laws regarding "Castle Doctrine").

In the context of "imminent threat of death or serious bodily harm," the word "imminent" refers to a danger that is **immediate and unavoidable** unless action is taken. It doesn't mean a potential or distant threat, but rather one that is happening right now or is about to occur with certainty.

An imminent threat is one where an attacker has the capability, opportunity, and intent to cause serious injury or death, leaving the victim with *no reasonable* option but to act in self-defense. For example, if an aggressor is brandishing a weapon, moving toward you with clear hostile intent, or physically attacking you, the threat is imminent because harm is about to happen unless it is stopped.

However, a verbal threat alone, or an individual who is angry but not actively engaging in violence, does not meet the standard of imminence. Understanding this distinction is *crucial*, as the legal justification for using force in self-defense can depend on the immediacy of the threat—if the danger is not truly imminent, the use of force may not be legally justified.

The Realities of a Physical Confrontation

Hollywood portrayals of violence are far from reality. In real life, fights are unpredictable, chaotic, and over in seconds.

What to Expect in a Real Fight

- **Adrenaline Dump:** Increased heart rate, shaking hands, and loss of fine motor skills.
- **Extreme Close Quarters:** Most violent encounters happen at arm's length or closer.
- **No Fair Fight:** Attackers do not fight fair. There are no rules, referees, or rounds.
- **Injury Is Inevitable:** Even in a successful defense, expect some level of injury.

The Purpose of Physical Violence in Self-Defense

The goal of using force in self-defense is not to "win" a fight but to create an incapacitating injury that *allows you to escape*. This means targeting areas that will immediately disrupt the attacker's ability to continue their assault.

In a situation where any of these options become necessary, it's critical to understand that this is literally a fight for your life—and not the time for half-hearted attempts. In order to create a **true incapacitation**, rather than simply enraging your attacker, you must commit yourself to extreme violence of action —channeling all of your strength and effort into a focused strike at a target of opportunity.

Incapacitating Targets

- **Eyes:** Gouging the eyes can disable an attacker instantly.
  Visualize driving your thumb into their eye socket and through the back of their head.

- **Throat:** Striking the throat can disrupt breathing and cause panic.
  Visualize driving your fist into their windpipe and through the back of their neck.

- **Knees:** A direct strike to the knee can collapse an attacker's stance and prevent pursuit.
  Visualize kicking their kneecap straight backward to at least a 45-degree angle.

- **Groin:** Although not always a fight-stopper, it can provide an opportunity to escape.
  Visualize kicking their testicles up into their chest cavity.

Training for Reality: Prepare to Survive

Relying on instinct alone is not enough. Training prepares the mind and body to act decisively under stress. In a potentially life-or-death situation, the stakes could not be higher … there is no "reset" button. You will have *one chance* for all the marbles. It's never a good idea to risk *everything* on your ability to do something that you'd never thought of—much less tried to do—before.

How to Train for Self-Defense

1. **Scenario-Based Drills:** Practicing real-life scenarios builds decision-making skills.

2. **Sparring and Resistance Training:** Facing live opponents increases confidence and adaptability.
3. **Weapons Training:** If carrying a firearm or non-lethal tool, train regularly to ensure proficiency.
4. **Stress "Inoculation":** Training under realistic conditions (simulated adrenaline, loud noises, surprise attacks) reduces hesitation in real confrontations.

Final Thoughts

Violence should never be the first choice, but when it becomes necessary, the ability to act decisively can mean survival. Whether using non-lethal tools, hand-to-hand combat, or a firearm, *preparation is key*. Remember—the goal is not to engage in prolonged combat, but to create an opportunity for escape by *incapacitating* the attacker.

If you're wondering where to start, the U.S. Concealed Carry Association offers a comprehensive lineup of online or in-person training opportunities of all types, many of which are free to attend. The thousands of USCCA Certified Instructors nationwide have been trained to offer practical and *legally-defensible* advice and guidance to help you along your personal security journey.

No matter what path you decide to take towards becoming a true stakeholder in your own safety and security, **train, stay aware, and be ready to act**—because in a crisis, hesitation can be fatal.

CHAPTER 8

Understanding the Consequences of Using Force

Using force in self-defense is often a split-second decision, but the ramifications can last a *lifetime*. Whether the force used is non-lethal or lethal, the aftermath almost always involves legal, civil, moral, and social considerations. Understanding these consequences in advance can help prepare you for what follows a self-defense incident.

Legal Ramifications: Are You Criminally Liable?

One of the most pressing concerns after a self-defense incident is *whether or not you will face criminal charges*. The legal system will scrutinize your actions to determine if your use of force was justified.

Was Your Use of Force Justified?

Most states follow some version of these principles:

- **Imminent Threat:** You must have *reasonably believed* you or another person was in immediate danger of bodily harm or death.

- **Proportionality:** The level of force used must *match* the threat. Deadly force is only justified against a threat that could reasonably cause death or serious bodily injury.

- **Duty to Retreat vs. Stand Your Ground:** Some states require individuals to *attempt to retreat* before using force. Other states, however, allow individuals to stand their ground if threatened.

- **Castle Doctrine:** Many states allow residents to use force to defend their homes (and in *some* cases, vehicles) without a duty to retreat.

If law enforcement determines that you acted in self-defense within the confines of the law, you *may* not face charges. It's absolutely critical that you know and understand the laws governing use-of-force and self-defense where you are. However, even justified self-defense cases can still result in criminal investigations, arrests, and multiple court appearances.

Civil Litigation: Will You Be Sued?

Even if you are cleared of criminal charges, *you may still face civil lawsuits from the attacker or their family.* Unlike criminal cases, where the burden of proof is "beyond a reasonable doubt," civil cases only require a "preponderance of evidence," making it far easier to be held liable.

Potential Civil Claims Against You

- **Wrongful Death Lawsuit:** If you used lethal force, the attacker's family may file a lawsuit claiming excessive or unnecessary force.

- **Personal Injury Lawsuit:** If the attacker survived but was injured, they could sue for damages, medical expenses, and lost wages. There are actual cases where a bystander has sued the person who lawfully defended themselves or others because they were traumatized by *witnessing* the violence.

- **Property Damage:** If your actions caused property damage, you might be held financially responsible.

How to Protect Yourself Legally

Photo by Delta Defense, LLC

Self-Defense Liability Insurance: Some organizations offer insurance that covers legal fees and damages related to self-defense incidents (more on this in Chapter 20). Having legal counsel that *specializes* in self-defense law *in your state* can be invaluable.

Document the Incident: Provide police with an accurate statement *after speaking with your attorney*, and ensure witnesses are identified to support your claim of self-defense.

Moral and Psychological Impact

Taking action in self-defense can be mentally and emotionally challenging. Even if justified, using force—especially lethal force—can have lasting moral and psychological consequences.

Common Psychological Responses

- **Survivor's Guilt:** Even when defending yourself, taking another life, or causing serious injury, can lead to guilt and emotional distress.
- **PTSD and Anxiety:** Witnessing or experiencing violence can cause long-term trauma.
- **Public Scrutiny and Judgment:** You may face criticism from those who weren't present or don't understand the circumstances.

How to Cope

- **Seek Professional Help:** Therapy or counseling can help process emotions and prevent long-term trauma.
- **Join Support Groups:** Connecting with others who have experienced similar situations can provide reassurance and advice.
- **Understand Your Decision:** Acknowledge and accept that self-defense was necessary to protect yourself or loved ones.

Social and Media Repercussions

In the modern digital age, self-defense incidents are often scrutinized in the court of public opinion before they are resolved legally. Social media, news outlets, and activists may *distort facts*, turning a justified self-defense situation into a controversy.

Potential Social Repercussions

- **Doxxing & Harassment:** Your personal information may be exposed online, leading to threats or job loss.
- **Media Bias:** The media may portray you in a negative light, regardless of the facts.
- **Community Backlash:** Friends, coworkers, and neighbors may have differing opinions about your actions.

- **Limit Public Statements:** Don't discuss the incident on social media; anything you say can be used against you legally or socially. Long before any potential incident happens, you should strongly consider how the "messaging" you post on social media *today* may affect how a potential jury member might perceive your "predisposition."

  Inflammatory proclamations such as "better to be judged by 12 than carried by 6" posted on your social media page long before a self-defense shooting may lead a jury to believe that you were *eager* to shoot someone ... certainly not helpful to your criminal defense attorney.

- **Work with Legal Counsel:** Your lawyer can help craft statements to minimize negative publicity. Other than the minimal statements to the police immediately following the incident outlined earlier, you should always consult your attorney prior to making any statements about the incident to anyone (not just law enforcement).

Know Your Rights

In the immediate aftermath of a self-defense incident, following a clear and structured response helps ensure both legal and personal safety. First, **secure the scene** by ensuring the immediate threat is neutralized and checking yourself and others for injuries. If it is safe to do so, holster or secure your firearm *before* law enforcement arrives to avoid any perception of ongoing danger.

Next, **call 911** and provide only the necessary information—state that there has been a self-defense incident, request medical assistance if needed, and identify yourself. When police arrive, comply with their commands, keep your hands visible, and avoid making any detailed statements beyond requesting legal representation.

The stress and adrenaline of the event can cloud memory, so it's crucial to **invoke your right to remain silent** and consult with an attorney before providing a full statement. Additionally, be prepared for emotional and psychological effects following a self-defense situation, and seek both legal and mental health support as needed.

Following these steps will help to ensure that you handle the situation responsibly while protecting your legal rights.

Final Thoughts

Using force in self-defense is never a decision to be taken lightly. The legal, civil, moral, and social ramifications can be significant. Understanding these factors *ahead of time* can help you make informed decisions and take necessary precautions.

While the right to self-defense is fundamental, ensuring you are legally, financially, and emotionally prepared for the aftermath is just as crucial. Be proactive—educate yourself, seek proper training, and have a legal plan in place. Your ability to protect yourself should extend beyond the fight itself to securing your future afterward.

CHAPTER 9

Developing *Your* Personal Security Plan

Why You Need a Personal Security Plan

A well-developed personal security plan ensures that you have proactive measures in place to reduce risk and respond quickly and effectively to threats. A comprehensive plan should address security at home, work, and in public while incorporating situational awareness, strategic positioning, and self-defense options.

The next few chapters will focus on developing a personal security plan for your **home**, while on the **road**, and while out in **public** or at **work**.

Staying Safe at Home: Fortification & Prevention

Your home should be your sanctuary. Unfortunately, in the U.S., a home burglary, or break-in, occurs **roughly every 26 seconds.**[6]

Strengthening your home's security reduces the likelihood of becoming a target and increases your ability to defend yourself if necessary. The *primary goal* here is to lead a criminal to look elsewhere for a potential break-in. Just as they usually select a victim to rob or assault who appears to be an easy, unprepared target, so too does this rule usually apply when selecting a home for a break-in.

You can significantly reduce the likelihood of a break-in by ensuring that your home appears to be a harder "nut to crack" than someplace else. This calculation reflects the stark reality that your mission is not to prevent a crime from happening, but rather to dissuade a criminal from selecting *your* home as their next target.

Any sound defensive strategy should incorporate **"layers" of defense.** Think of concentric rings, starting from well outside of your home, working inwards towards what is most important: you and your loved ones. The security measures within these rings should become *increasingly more apparent and robust* the closer they get to you.

The example below is for a stand-alone, single-family home in a typical suburban neighborhood. You can adapt these concepts and principles to your particular home setting, no matter where you live.

First Impressions Matter

Start from the street, viewing your home from a burglar's perspective. Maintaining the exterior of your home is crucial in deterring potential burglaries, as a well-kept property signals that the house is occupied and regularly monitored.

Overgrown bushes, poor lighting, and neglected maintenance can create hiding spots for intruders and suggest that a home may be an easy target. Installing motion-sensor lights, trimming hedges near windows and doors,

---

[6]FBI, Crime in the U.S. 2019.

and ensuring that doors, fences, and locks are in good condition can *significantly* reduce the likelihood of a break-in.

A **visible security system**, such as cameras or alarm signs, also serves as a powerful deterrent. By keeping the exterior of your home tidy, secure, and well-lit, you not only enhance its curb appeal but also improve its overall safety, protecting both your property and your loved ones.

Home Security Checklist

Does the home look well-maintained?

- Is the yard well-maintained?
- Are the trees and bushes trimmed back to ensure open sightlines and remove potential hiding places?

Does the home appear to be occupied? Contrary to popular belief, *most burglaries occur during daylight hours[7],* when residents are likely away. These simple tips can make a big difference:

- A car in the driveway that doesn't look like it's been parked for weeks.
- Lights on inside (timers are great, but older versions are a known fire hazard).
- Keep windows and doors closed and locked, even when you are home. If you use window screens, consider upgrading to a stainless steel mesh instead of easy-to-cut fabric.
- Make sure to stop mail, newspaper, and package deliveries, or ask a trusted neighbor to collect them each day. A stack of uncollected newspapers or packages is a good indicator that the homeowner is away.

---

[7] FBI UCR

Securing the Exterior of Your Home: Think Like a Burglar

While it's nearly impossible to make your home completely impenetrable, there are several simple and relatively inexpensive ways to significantly increase its security.

Remember: "Builder's Grade" indicates that the materials (doors, hardware, etc) used were likely the most affordable *for the builder*—and not necessarily of the best or most robust quality. Upgrading to a higher quality deadbolt lock and longer mounting screws will go a long way towards fortifying your doors. Glass in and around doors or on windows should be reinforced with a security laminate.

The goal here is to keep someone from easily breaking the glass and reaching through to open the lock. Security barrier devices are a great addition to any door, preventing someone from being able to enter with one swift kick. Again, these devices may not hold up indefinitely, but if properly installed, they will almost certainly *buy you the time* you need to react and defend yourself effectively.

Upgrade Door Materials

- Use solid-core or metal instead of hollow-core construction on all exterior doors and select interior doors.
- Consider doors with reinforced steel or fiberglass for maximum security.

Strengthen the Door Frame

- Replace the standard door frame with a reinforced steel or heavy-duty wood frame.
- Use a security strike plate with at least 3-inch screws to anchor it into the wall stud.
- Install a door reinforcement kit to strengthen weak points.

Improve Locking Mechanisms

- Install a high-quality deadbolt (ANSI Grade 1 or 2) with a 1-inch throw bolt.
- Use a reinforced strike plate with long screws to prevent forceful entry.
- Consider double-cylinder deadbolts for doors with glass panels (check local codes for compliance).

Enhance Door Hinges

- Replace standard hinge screws with 3-inch screws to anchor into the wall stud.
- Use security hinges or hinge pins to prevent removal from the outside.

Add Additional Security Features

- Install a reinforced door bar or door barricade for extra resistance against forced entry.
- Use a door reinforcement lock (such as a night latch or swing bar lock).
- Place door security film on glass panels to prevent easy break-ins.

Install a Peephole or Doorbell Camera

- Use a wide-angle peephole or "door scope" to see outside without opening the door.
- Install a video doorbell or security camera for real-time monitoring.

Ensure Proper Lighting and Visibility

- Install motion-activated lights near entryways to deter intruders.
- Keep landscaping trimmed to avoid providing cover for potential burglars.

Test Your Security Measures Regularly

- Check locks, hinges, and reinforcement hardware for wear and tear.
- Perform periodic security drills to ensure all household members know emergency procedures.

Securing the Interior of Your Home: Think Like a SWAT Operator

"**Speed, Surprise**, and **Violence of Action**" are core tenets of effective tactical operations, emphasizing swift, overwhelming actions to gain dominance and minimize the opposition's ability to react. As a SWAT team member, my team and I relied upon these principles to greatly enhance our odds of success while attempting to arrest a bad guy.

These same principles apply to violent criminals. They know that if they can take their intended victim by surprise, quickly overwhelming them (both physically and psychologically), they can almost certainly preclude any meaningful resistance.

Think of these principles as comprising a "three legged stool"—if any one of the three principles fails (you *don't* take the target by surprise, you *don't* move fast enough to exploit that surprise, or you *don't* act with sufficient force) the stool collapses and the odds of success are greatly reduced. As the potential victim of violence, you're only in a position to affect one of these "legs." In designing your home security plan, the overarching goal should be to *never be taken by surprise.*

Remember—early detection and avoidance are paramount in any sound security plan. The "home hardening" recommendations above may not indefinitely preclude a determined attacker from gaining access to your home, but they will present significant resistance to that entry. The extra effort—and noise—created by the presence of these security barriers will buy you that most precious of resources during an emergency: **TIME.**

Rather than being taken completely by surprise as someone kicks in your front door and is upon you before you can even process what is happening, these extra few seconds may afford you and your loved ones the time you need to react effectively. The time you need to retreat to a *prepared*, defensive position—behind another sturdy barricade, armed, and ready to defend yourself if necessary. Once you're there, call 911 and get help on the way.

How to Select and Equip a "Panic" or "Holdfast" Room in Your Home

Long ago, when danger threatened, people retreated to the safety of a "holdfast"—a place where they could secure themselves and protect the ones they loved **until help arrived or the crisis passed**. Although daily life has changed considerably since the Middle Ages, the basic concepts and principles of personal safety and security have not. The ability to quickly put *time and distance* between yourself and a sudden, unexpected threat is often the deciding factor in a crisis.

A bit of forethought, planning, and strategic positioning of defensive measures can help ensure that you and your loved ones achieve a positive outcome. There is no time like the present to begin planning, establishing, and discussing your family's home security emergency plan. Begin with thoughtfully selecting a holdfast room in your home with the following in mind:

Minimal Entry Points

- Choose a room with only one entrance.
- Choose a room that is easily and quickly accessible from key areas
  of the house where you typically spend the most time
  (e.g., bedrooms or the living room).
- Ensure all family members can reach it within seconds in an emergency.
- Avoid rooms with multiple external walls or excess windows, which can be breached more easily.

Structural Strength

- Opt for an interior room with strong walls, such as a bedroom, closet, basement, or storage room.
- If possible, select a room with concrete, brick, or reinforced walls for added protection.
- Avoid rooms with weak doors or large windows.
- Select a room with one entry point to control access more effectively. This will serve to "channel" your attacker(s) into a single, narrow entrance that can be more effectively defended.

If you have the means to do so, consider these upgrades:

- **Door:** Install an inward-opening, solid-core or steel door with a heavy-duty deadbolt.
  Reinforce the door with an additional barricade device such as a security door bar.
- **Walls:** Reinforce with steel plates, Kevlar panels, or concrete for extra protection.
- **Windows:** If windows are present, use bullet-resistant glass or added security laminate.

Communication & Connectivity

- Ensure cell phone signals work inside the room, or have a landline installed.
- Choose a room where you can install a hidden camera feed or intercom system.
- Make sure there's an electrical outlet for charging emergency

devices or powering security equipment.

Ventilation & Comfort

- Select a room that allows adequate airflow or can be equipped with a separate ventilation system.
- If possible, ensure temperature control so the room remains comfortable during extended stays.
- Choose a room with enough space to store emergency supplies, such as food, water, and medical kits.

Entry & Escape Options

- Ideally, the room should have a concealed secondary exit, such as an attic hatch or hidden door.
- If an exit isn't feasible, make sure the room is fortified well enough to withstand threats until help arrives.

Essential Supplies

- **Food & Water:** Stock at least 72 hours' worth of supplies.
- **First-Aid Kit:** Include medical supplies, medications, and basic wound care items.
- **Flashlights & Batteries:** Keep emergency lighting available.
- **Self-Defense Items:** Depending on local laws, consider pepper spray, a firearm, or other protective equipment.

Final Thoughts

Securing your home isn't just about locks, alarms, or hardware—it's about adopting a mindset that values preparedness over panic. Thinking like a SWAT operator doesn't mean gearing up for war; it means respecting *how quickly* violence can unfold and building layers of defense that deny an attacker the element of surprise.

Every lock, barricade, or reinforced door you install is a silent investment in your family's survival time. A well-prepared holdfast room isn't a sign of paranoia, it's a sign of foresight. The moments you buy with early warning, strategic planning, and thoughtful layout could mean the difference between being a victim and being ready. Your home should not only be your sanctuary—it should also be your stronghold.

CHAPTER 10

Staying Safe On The Road: Defensive Driving & Threat Mitigation

For most, our roadway journeys bring us into closer contact with a wider cross-section of the population than at any other time in our daily lives. At any given moment on the road, you could be seated *just feet away* from a violent predator with nothing but a single pane of glass between you. Yet for many, the time spent in a car is often deeply distracted in thought, conversation, or electronic media—lulled into a false sense of security, seated and strapped into a small, glass-enclosed box.

As a member of an Executive Protection team, I knew that any "transitional" movements (moving from one relatively controlled and secured space to another, e.g., from a home to an office) were times of maximum vulnerability. In fact, the majority of assassination attempts occur in close proximity to a vehicle. Remember—**what is predictable is exploitable.**

It's easy to predict where someone will be if you know where they'll be getting into or out of a car (think of the paparazzi waiting for a movie star to exit their limousine). This principle applies to all of us. If someone knows what car you drive, they can predict with certainty where you will likely be at some point later today. Some of us are "lucky" enough to have a designated parking spot at work, with a name plate on a sign reserving the spot, making this type of prediction that much easier.

Movement in public significantly reduces the control you have over *proximity and access* others may have to you. This is why you see dignitaries travel via motorcade, often involving several vehicles and multiple protection team members. Most of the planning and coordination work done by an executive protection team is related to movement. Accordingly, this is when those of us who don't have the luxury of a security detail need to remain more vigilant.

No one can remain hyper-vigilant for long in any circumstance, so we need to understand when to pay extra attention during times of increased vulnerability and exposure to potential threats. When traveling at speed on the interstate, while there is certainly a threat from a reckless driver or other roadway hazard, there is very little chance that someone will attempt a carjacking. But when stopped in traffic or at a red light, you are perilously vulnerable.

A predator can predict with absolute certainty where an almost endless procession of potential victims will be—seated, motionless for minutes at a time, stopped at a red light. This is not the time to be checking your smartphone. The following concepts and principles will significantly increase your personal security when on the road.

Vehicle Security Tips

- **Doors Locked at All Times:** Keep doors locked and windows rolled up when stopped.

- **Keep a Safe Distance:** Don't allow yourself to be "boxed in." Maintain enough space between your vehicle and the one in front at stops to allow for an **escape route**.

  In an extreme emergency, don't hesitate to drive off the roadway or to ram a blocking vehicle to escape a violent confrontation. *Be prepared for airbag deployment.*

  Front airbags are designed to deploy in frontal or near-frontal collisions of ~14 mph or higher, typically within a 30-degree angle on either side of the vehicle's centerline. While only advisable in an extreme emergency, most cars can still be driven after airbag deployment.

- **Situational Awareness While Stopped:** Maintain awareness of what is happening around your vehicle. Watch for someone approaching on foot and be prepared to drive away quickly.

- **Situational Awareness in Parking Lots:** Park in well-lit areas with open sight lines around your vehicle, scan your surroundings before entering or exiting your car, and avoid distractions during this highly vulnerable time.

If something doesn't look right, be prepared to find another parking spot or, if you are walking to your car, turn around and go ask for someone to escort you.

- **Avoid Predictable Driving Routes:** Vary your daily commute to reduce targeting by criminals.

  Identify areas along your commute (close to your house or work) where someone could plausibly stay for long periods of time without arousing suspicion (e.g., a bus stop, park bench, coffee shop, etc). These areas are favorites of criminals who may be conducting surveillance.

- **Be Aware of "Bump & Rob" Tactics:** Criminals may cause minor accidents to lure victims out of their vehicles. Be prepared to drive away from the scene. If you're at all suspicious, relate that you will drive to a local police station parking lot to exchange insurance information.

- **Keep Valuables Out Of Sight:** This helps prevent smash-and-grab thefts. If confronted, prioritize your safety over material possessions.

- **Maintain a Charged Phone:** Make sure it's pre-programmed with emergency contacts.

- **Concealed Weapons:** Keep self-defense tools handy if legally permitted.

- **Fuel Up in Safe Locations:** Preferably during the day in busy areas rather than isolated gas stations. Busy, multi-pump locations are usually much safer than small, isolated gas stations, especially if you need to go inside for any reason.

  Keep in mind, someone using the restroom in a small, isolated gas station is incredibly vulnerable (literally "getting caught with their pants down").

Responding to Threats While Driving

- **Avoid Road Rage Incidents:** *Never* engage aggressive drivers—your priority is avoidance or de-escalation. You have no way of knowing who the other driver is or what level of violence they are prepared to escalate to. Be comfortable with "swallowing your pride" in order to get on with the rest of your day. Road rage incidents never end well.

- **Escape When Possible:** If you suspect you're being followed, drive to a police station or populated area. Phone ahead to have someone step out and meet you if possible.

- **Carjacking:** If confronted, assess the situation—if the criminal demands your car and your wallet, surrender them and move away. These *things* can all be replaced, and doing so will almost certainly not be as disruptive to your life as engaging in a use-of-force incident would be.

  If feasible, toss your wallet off to one side and the car keys in another direction—then quickly move away. **But if they try to force you to go with them, or to another location, do everything you can to escape.**

Someone who is threatening to harm you unless you "go with them quietly" is not someone who should be trusted to uphold their end of the bargain.

Remember—in a situation like this, they're trying to quietly move you to a location more conducive to their plans, *where no one else is likely to intervene.* If they had simply wanted to hurt or kill you, they would have done so when they first surprised you. Acquiescence in this circumstance will only make it less likely to end well for you.

Your vehicle is an extension of your security environment. When driving, maintaining personal security is crucial to avoid potential threats and dangerous situations. Understanding defensive driving techniques reduces vulnerability to crime and accidents. Always keep your **doors locked** and windows rolled up when stopped, especially in unfamiliar or high-crime areas.

Stay aware of your surroundings, avoiding distractions like excessive phone use, and be mindful of vehicles following you for an extended period. If you suspect you're being followed, drive to a well-lit, busy area or a *police station* rather than heading home. Park in **well-lit** areas and scan your surroundings before exiting or entering your vehicle.

If someone approaches your car in a suspicious manner, do not engage, **drive away** if possible. Avoid stopping for strangers on the road; instead, call emergency services if someone appears in distress.

Keep valuables out of sight to prevent smash-and-grab thefts, and if confronted, prioritize your safety over material possessions. In case of an emergency, have a charged phone and emergency contacts readily available, and consider carrying self-defense tools like pepper spray if legal in your area. Staying alert and taking these precautions can *significantly* reduce your risk of becoming a target while on the road.

Final Thoughts

Personal security doesn't end at your front door, it travels with you. Your vehicle is a mobile extension of your personal environment, and the time you spend in it is often when you're most exposed.

Whether commuting to work, running errands, or driving across town, your predictability, your routines, and your level of awareness can all be exploited by someone with bad intentions. By adopting a mindset rooted in **intentional movement, situational awareness, and controlled unpredictability**, you dramatically reduce your vulnerability.

You don't need to live in fear, but you *do need* to live prepared. Defensive driving isn't just about avoiding accidents—it's about thinking one step ahead, identifying potential threats before they unfold, and knowing when to disengage, de-escalate, or act. Make vigilance your habit, not your exception, and ensure that wherever the road takes you, you stay in control of your safety.

CHAPTER 11

Staying Safe in Public

Strategic Positioning & Awareness

Where you position yourself in public spaces significantly impacts your ability to detect and respond to threats.

Whenever I first enter a building, I make a habit of seeking out the restroom with the pretense of washing my hands. This allows me to observe the interior layout as well as the people and activity inside while noting exits and other potential egress routes. This also allows me to select where I want to sit to remain situationally aware while there. I'm willing to wait a little longer for a preferred table and empower myself to do so.

Restaurants & Coffee Shops

- Sit where you can see the entrance while maintaining a view of the entire room.

- Position yourself near an exit for easy escape if necessary.
- Avoid sitting with your back to the door.

Movie Theaters, Houses of Worship, & Large Venues

- Choose an aisle seat near an exit for fast evacuation.
- Be aware of emergency exits before the event begins.
- Identify unusual behavior around you and be prepared to move if necessary.

Public Transportation

- Stand or sit near the driver or conductor.
- Avoid empty train cars or bus sections, especially at night.
- Be alert when using ride-share services; confirm vehicle details before entering.

Shopping Centers & Malls

- Avoid becoming distracted while shopping—criminals look for inattentive targets.
- Be aware of people loitering in parking lots or near your vehicle.
- Be prepared to push through the "Employees Only" door at the back of the store—most stores have a rear exit that opens onto a service hallway or to the outside.

"Courtesy" vs. Safety

Returning your grocery cart to the designated corral may seem like a simple act of courtesy, but it also carries implications for personal security, *especially when children are involved*. Leaving your vehicle to return the cart, even for a brief moment, can create a window of vulnerability. If you have young children with you, **never leave them unattended** in the car while you do so; not only is this unsafe, but it may also be illegal in many jurisdictions.

Instead, if you're alone with your kids, consider parking close to a cart corral when you arrive so you can return the cart without straying from your vehicle. Otherwise, *empower yourself* to be "discourteous" by not returning the cart.

Staying aware of your surroundings and prioritizing the safety of your children over social niceties is key. Personal security often hinges on small decisions, and minimizing time spent distracted or separated from your dependents in public places is always a smart move.

Final Thoughts

Public spaces introduce a unique set of security challenges—chief among them is your lack of control over who is near you and what their intentions may be. While you can't control the environment, you can absolutely control how you engage with it.

Strategic positioning, subtle observation, and deliberate movement all give you a *distinct advantage* over someone who is simply drifting through the day unaware. By making a habit of scanning for exits, choosing seats that offer visibility and access, and recognizing unusual behavior before it becomes a threat, you dramatically increase your chances of avoiding or surviving a dangerous encounter.

These practices don't require paranoia—they require presence. With just a bit of forethought and vigilance, you can **move confidently** through public spaces while keeping your personal safety firmly in your own hands.

CHAPTER 12

Staying Safe at Work

Developing a Personal Security Plan on the Job

For many of us, the workplace is where we spend the majority of our waking hours. Whether you're in an office building, a retail environment, a school, a warehouse, or on the road, the potential for encountering violence, emergencies, or other security threats is real—and often overlooked.

Many people assume that their employer is solely responsible for workplace safety. While most organizations do have basic safety policies and procedures in place, they may not be enough to address **personal threats, active violence, or targeted aggression.**

The truth is, your safety at work is ultimately your responsibility. A well-developed personal security plan tailored to *your specific work environment* can make the difference between being a victim and achieving a positive outcome during a critical event.

Know Your Environment

The first step in developing a workplace security plan is understanding the physical and social layout of your work environment. Begin with these foundational questions:

- Where are the exits?
- Are there alternate ways out if the main route is blocked?
- Do doors lock from the inside or outside?
- Are there designated safe rooms, secure areas, or concealed spaces?
- What areas are isolated, poorly lit, or lack surveillance coverage?

Spend a few minutes mentally mapping your primary workspace, break areas, restrooms, parking lot, and any connecting hallways or stairwells. Pay special attention to areas where visibility is limited or where someone could hide.

Understanding these spaces will help you form an effective plan for escape, concealment, or defense in the event of a crisis.

Assess Potential Threats

Different jobs carry different risks. A retail worker may be concerned about robberies. A healthcare provider might worry about aggressive patients or family members. An office worker could be vulnerable to domestic violence threats that follow them to the workplace. Consider the specific risks you face based on your **industry, role, location, and public access.**

Be honest with yourself:

- Do you work alone or with others?
- Is your name publicly displayed or easily searchable?
- Do angry customers or clients visit or have access to your workplace?
- Have there been previous security incidents at your job site?

Once you understand your threat profile, you can begin taking steps to reduce exposure and improve readiness.

Establish a Baseline

Just as in public spaces, establishing a baseline of normal activity at work helps you quickly identify when something feels "off." Learn the routine of your environment—how people usually move, talk, and behave throughout the day. When someone deviates from that norm (loitering, nervous behavior, entering areas they shouldn't), *take note of it*. Intuition is a powerful early warning system. Don't ignore it just because you're in a familiar place.

Have a Plan for Active Threats

Active shooter incidents and workplace violence are rare, but they do happen. And when they do, they unfold fast. You may only have seconds to respond. Here's a basic framework to follow, often referred to as **Avoid, Deny, Defend** (similar to Run, Hide, Fight):

- **Avoid:** If you can escape safely, do it *immediately*.
  Know your exits and be prepared to use them.
- **Deny:** If you *can't* escape, lock and barricade the door.
  Turn off lights, silence phones, and remain quiet.
- **Defend:** If you're confronted and escape is impossible, be
  prepared to use whatever force is necessary to protect your life.

  Use whatever improvised weapons are available—
  fire extinguishers, scissors, furniture. Remember, don't make this
  a "fair" fight. If possible, *coordinate with others* to employ **Speed,
  Surprise, and Violence of Action** to quickly incapacitate the
  attacker.

Designate rally points with trusted coworkers, and have a communication plan if cell service goes down. Know who to contact and where to meet after an incident.

Protect Your Personal Information

Many security threats are enabled by easy access to personal information. In the workplace:

- Keep ID badges secured when not in use.
- Avoid displaying full names on office directories if not required.
- Limit social media posts that reveal your schedule, location, or routine.
- Be cautious about giving out personal contact information to clients or customers.
- Know how to recognize phishing emails or social engineering attempts.
- Your privacy is part of your personal security. Guard it accordingly.

Be Security-Minded in the Parking Lot

Parking lots and garages are frequent sites of workplace assaults and robberies due to limited visibility and predictable foot traffic. Maintain awareness when walking to and from your vehicle:

- Walk with purpose, head up, phone down.
- Keep keys in hand and check your surroundings before approaching your vehicle.

- Park in well-lit areas and avoid isolated spots when possible.
- If you feel uneasy, ask for a security escort or walk out with a coworker.

Remember—your vulnerability increases during transitions—*especially* when entering or exiting your vehicle.

Prepare a Workplace Go-Bag

Just as you might keep emergency supplies at home or in your car, consider creating a discreet **workplace go-bag** that contains essentials in case you need to shelter in place or evacuate. Consider including:

- Flashlight and batteries
- Emergency contact list
- Small first-aid kit
- Phone charger and power bank
- Bottled water and snacks
- Spare keys
- Self-defense tool (where legal and permitted)
- Cash or transportation card

Keep this bag accessible but out of plain sight—perhaps in a drawer, locker, or under your desk.

Engage with Your Employer

If your workplace lacks a formal security plan, or if you notice gaps in the existing one, consider raising the issue constructively. Offer to be part of a safety committee or suggest hosting a workplace safety workshop. Encourage conversations around emergency drills, access control, and communication protocols. The goal isn't to instill fear but to build a culture of **shared responsibility** for safety.

Final Thoughts

Just as with your home or vehicle, your workplace should be part of your personal security footprint. Most people spend more time at work than anywhere else, so prepare accordingly.

Know your environment, understand your risks, and have a plan. Be aware, be proactive, and build layers of defense that allow you to respond with clarity and purpose if something goes wrong. Safety on the job doesn't come from wishful thinking, it comes from *intentional* action.

CHAPTER 13

Building a Security Plan With Your School-Aged Child

As a parent, there is no greater priority than the safety of your children. In today's world, preparing your school-aged child with a personal security plan is not just wise—it's *essential*.

Whether they're navigating their school day, interacting online, or encountering unfamiliar adults, children need tools, confidence, and guidance to make smart, safe choices.

This chapter will walk you through how to build a simple, effective security plan with your child, including specific actions for active shooter scenarios, social media awareness, and interactions with strangers.

Start With a Conversation, Not a Lecture

The first step is to create an open dialogue. Kids are more likely to engage and remember what they're taught if they feel like part of the process. Ask questions like:

- "What would you do if something scary happened at school?"
- "Do you know who to talk to if someone online makes you uncomfortable?"
- "What do you think is safe or unsafe when meeting someone new?"

Make it clear that the goal isn't to scare them, but to prepare them. Just like we practice fire drills or look both ways before crossing the street, personal security is about smart habits that keep us safe.

All children need a trusted adult in their lives, and it's critical that you remain one of them. As with any inter-personal relationship, we develop and **sustain the trust** of our school-aged child by consistently listening without judgment, following through on promises, and creating a safe space where questions, fears, and mistakes are met with patience and support.

Planning for an Active Shooter Scenario

No parent wants to imagine violence unfolding in the halls of their child's school, but for today's children, that threat is a constant presence in their consciousness. It wasn't always this way. In the first five years after the FBI began formally tracking active shooter incidents, the U.S. averaged roughly six qualifying attacks per year.

By 2021, that number had climbed to 61—a staggering **900% increase** in the two decades since Columbine.[8] For children growing up in this era, active shooter drills, lockdown procedures, and scanning for exits in public spaces are as normal as fire drills were a generation ago.

---

[8]Federal Bureau of Investigation, Active Shooter Incidents in the United States in 2023 (Washington, DC: U.S. Department of Justice, 2024), https://www.fbi.gov/file-repository/reports-and-publications/2023-active-shooter-report-062124.pdf/view.

If you graduated prior to 1999, it might be hard to fully appreciate just how deeply this has altered a child's mindset. I still remember a hot day late in the school year when the power went out in my classroom. My classmates and I cheered, knowing it meant an early dismissal.

That same thing happened recently where my daughter teaches at a public middle school. But this time, when the lights cut out, the cafeteria full of kids didn't erupt in joy. Instead, it was filled with shrieks of fear. Each child instinctively assumed the blackout was the beginning of an attack.

This heartbreaking anxiety is part of their daily lives. And while we can't erase it, we can help manage it. As a trusted adult, your presence, guidance, and willingness to have uncomfortable but necessary conversations can provide **real peace of mind**. By acknowledging these low-probability but ultra-high-consequence events and giving your child practical strategies to face them, you help *transform fear into preparedness*.

Preparing your child for the unthinkable isn't easy—but it's necessary. Today's school-aged kids face a vastly different reality from previous generations. While this is a difficult topic to discuss, doing so from a place of calm, care, and readiness can significantly reduce fear and increase your child's ability to respond effectively in a crisis.

As a parent, your job is to guide and empower your child through honest conversations and practical preparation. Knowing what to expect, having clear steps to follow, and building confidence in their ability to respond are all crucial parts of the equation.

What You Can Do:

- **Understand your child's school's active shooter plan:** Request a copy or attend safety briefings if available. Ask how drills are conducted, what lockdown procedures are in place, and what role teachers play. Go over these procedures with your child so they understand what to expect and how they fit into the plan.

- **Talk about the real risk:** Share age-appropriate facts about the frequency of these events and why being prepared matters. Avoid sensationalism, but don't avoid the conversation.

- **Introduce the "Run, Hide, Fight" strategy:** This mantra is widely taught and easy to recall under stress. Explain each response in simple terms:

  1. Run: If it's possible to escape, they should do so immediately and keep moving until they reach safety.

  2. Hide: If they can't run, they should hide out of sight, silence devices, and lock or barricade doors if possible.

  3. Fight: As a last resort, if directly confronted, they may need to use anything available to defend themselves long enough to escape.

- **Empower independent thinking:** Teach your child that while listening to teachers and law enforcement is important, *they may need to make quick decisions on their own.* Help them develop "premade decisions" that they can fall back on in a crisis.

- **Normalize practice:** Just like a fire drill, rehearsing responses builds muscle memory. Walk through what they might do in various scenarios—at school, in the cafeteria, or on the playground. Keep the tone serious but supportive.

- **Give permission to act:** Make it clear that their safety comes first. Let them know it's okay to break a rule or a window to escape *if they truly believe they are in danger.* Tell them you support their decision to act, even if it turns out to be a false alarm.

By replacing fear with action and anxiety with understanding, you give your child not only a plan—but peace of mind.

Social Media & Digital Safety

Today's threats don't just come through doors—they come through screens. From cyberbullying to predators, your child's online activity should be part of their security plan.

Key Lessons:

- **Never share personal information:** Teach them to avoid posting their full name, address, school name, or daily schedule.

- **Disable geo-location** tagging on photos and videos - most smartphones automatically include "hidden" data in photos and videos, making it easy for predators to pinpoint where the recording was made.

- **Privacy settings are a must:** Help them set their profiles to private and explain the importance of controlling who sees their content.

- **Think before you post:** Explain that once something is online, it can't truly be erased.

- **Recognize red flags:** Any adult messaging them out of the blue, asking for secrecy, or requesting photos is a major warning sign. They should tell a parent immediately.

Make time to periodically review their apps and accounts together. Be respectful, but be involved.

Interacting With Unknown Adults

Whether at school, in a park, or on the way home, your child needs to be equipped to handle interactions with adults they don't know.

Teach Boundaries:

- Adults don't ask kids for help: Reinforce that if an adult asks them for directions, help finding a pet, or a ride somewhere, they should walk away and find a trusted adult.

- "No" is a complete sentence: Give your child permission to say no, walk away, and seek help, even if the adult seems nice or polite.

- Have a family code word: This is a secret word or phrase only you and your child know. If someone claims they were sent by a parent, they must know the password.

- Know who "safe adults" are: Teachers, uniformed police officers, or another parent with children can be considered safe points of contact.

Building the Plan Together

Here's how to formalize your child's personal security plan:

1. **Emergency contacts:** Ensure they know how to reach you and at least one other trusted adult.

2. **Memorize key details:** Full name, home address, phone number.

3. **Safe words:** For pick-ups, online messages, or any situation requiring confirmation.

4. **Map routes:** Know their path to and from school, and identify safe spots along the way.

5. **Role-play scenarios:** Practice how to respond to emergencies, suspicious behavior, or unsafe online interactions. Empower your child to act in their own best interest if they feel threatened.

6. **Check-ins:** Set times to connect after school or activities.

7. **Reunification plan:** Develop a family reunification plan in case of a major disruption in communications (e.g., "If phone service is out for an extended period and you're not sure what to do, get to the house and wait for me there.").

Final Thoughts

Empowering your child with a security plan isn't about instilling fear—it's about fostering awareness, confidence, and resilience. Just like we train on the range, situational preparedness begins with **intentional conversations** and practical training.

When a child knows they have a plan, they don't just feel safer—they *are* safer.

Your job as a protector doesn't stop at the front door. It extends into the classroom, the digital world, and every space your child explores. Stay involved. Stay informed. And most of all, stay ready.

CHAPTER 14

Staying Safe On a College Campus

College is an exciting time filled with new experiences, friendships, and opportunities. However, young adults (ages 18-24) are more likely to be victims of serious violent crime than any other age group, so ensuring personal safety on campus is just as important as academic success.[9] By being aware of potential risks and taking proactive measures, students can create a safer environment for themselves and their peers. This chapter provides practical strategies for staying safe while navigating college life.

1. Understand Your Campus Environment

- Familiarize yourself with the layout of your campus, including emergency exits, blue light emergency phones, and security offices.
- Be aware of campus crime statistics and reports, which are often

---

[9]Bureau of Justice Statistics, Age Patterns of Victims of Serious Violent Crimes, NCJ 314832 (Washington, DC: U.S. Department of Justice, 2023), https://bjs.ojp.gov/content/pub/pdf/apvsvc.pdf.

available on the college's website or through campus security.

- Get to know the safest routes to and from your residence, classes, and common areas, especially if you need to walk alone at night. Don't hesitate to participate in the campus safety escort program if available.
- Enroll in your college campus emergency notification system. Make sure notifications are enabled.

2. Residence Hall and Apartment Safety

- Keep your dorm room or apartment door locked at all times. Use a security door bar for added security.
- Don't allow strangers or unverified guests into residence halls or apartment complexes. Remember—not holding the door for someone isn't rude, it's what's safest for everyone.
- If you live off-campus, ensure that doors and windows have secure locks, and consider installing security devices like door alarms or cameras.
- Report suspicious activity to campus security or local law enforcement immediately.

3. Personal Safety While Walking on Campus

- Avoid walking alone at night whenever possible. Use campus security escort services or walk with friends.
- Stay in well-lit, populated areas and avoid shortcuts through dark or isolated spaces.
- Keep your phone charged and accessible in case of an emergency, but avoid distractions such as texting or wearing both earbuds while walking.
- Carry a personal safety alarm, pepper spray, or other personal safety device if allowed by campus policy.

4. Transportation Safety

- Use campus shuttle services, rideshare apps, or trusted friends for transportation, especially at night.
- Verify the identity of rideshare drivers before getting into a vehicle by checking the car's license plate and driver's information on the app.
- If using public transportation, wait in well-lit areas and be aware

of your surroundings.

- Always lock your car and avoid leaving valuables visible inside.

5. Party and Social Event Safety

- Attend parties and social gatherings with friends and look out for one another. Arrive and leave together.
- Never accept drinks from strangers or leave your drink unattended.
- Be aware of the signs of alcohol poisoning and drug use, and seek help if you or someone else is in distress.
- Understand the impact of alcohol and drugs on your judgment and vulnerability. Know your limits and empower yourself to exit any situation that makes you uncomfortable.

6. Online and Digital Safety

- Protect personal information by using strong passwords and enabling multi-factor authentication on accounts.
- Avoid real-time location sharing on social media platforms.
- Do not share personal details with strangers online, especially through dating apps or social networking sites.
- Report any cyberbullying, stalking, or harassment to campus security and local authorities.

7. Building a Safety Network

- Keep emergency contacts programmed into your phone, including campus security, local law enforcement, and trusted friends or family members.
- Establish a system with friends where you check in with each other when going out or arriving home safely.
- Join campus safety programs, self-defense classes, or safety workshops to increase confidence and preparedness.

8. Responding to Emergencies

- Trust your instincts—if something feels off, *remove yourself* from the situation.
- If you feel threatened, move to a populated area and call for help immediately.

- Learn the locations of emergency call stations and how to quickly access campus security.
- If you're a victim of a crime, *report it* as soon as possible and seek support from campus resources, such as counseling services.

Final Thoughts

Staying safe on a college campus requires a combination of awareness, preparedness, and community vigilance. By taking these precautions and staying informed about campus safety resources, students can create a secure and enjoyable college experience. Safety is a *shared responsibility*, and by looking out for yourself and others, you can contribute to a safer campus environment for all.

CHAPTER 15

Defensive Tools

Including **defensive tools** in your personal security plan is not about seeking conflict—it's about ensuring you have the means to survive and prevail if one is forced upon you. Just as you wouldn't prepare for a fire without a fire extinguisher, you shouldn't prepare for personal threats without a reliable means of self-defense.

Your choice of self-defense tools depends on legal and policy considerations, personal comfort, and training level. Whether it's a firearm, a non-lethal option, or an improvised tool, having access to something you've trained with and can deploy effectively under stress is essential. Defensive tools extend your ability to respond decisively when escape or de-escalation are no longer options.

Selecting the right tool for your environment, comfort level, and legal land-scape is key—but more important than the tool itself is your mindset and readiness to use it responsibly. Tools don't keep you safe—*trained people with the right tools do.*

Non-Lethal Self-Defense Options

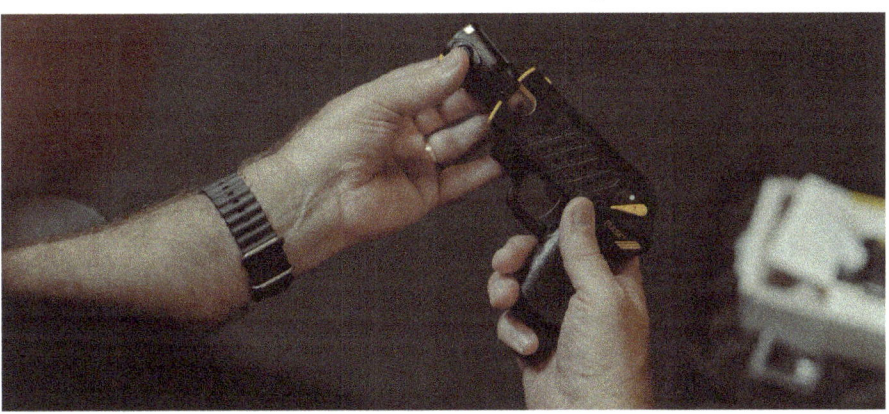

Photo by Delta Defense, LLC

These defensive tools are not designed to cause long-term, serious bodily injury or death. Sometimes referred to as "Less Than Lethal," it should be understood that these are weapons and can, in rare cases, cause severe injury or *even death*. The decision to use them must be seriously considered and legally justified.

In general, the **legal requirement** to use a non-lethal weapon is the same as for any other form of self-defense: you must reasonably believe you are in imminent danger of harm to yourself or others, and the force used must be *proportionate* to the threat.

- **Pepper Spray:** Effective at close range, causing temporary blindness and pain.
- **Tasers/Stun Guns:** Can incapacitate an attacker but require close proximity.
- **Kubotans & Tactical Pens:** Small impact weapons useful for striking pressure points.
- **Personal Alarms:** Loud sounds to attract attention and deter attackers.

Lethal Self-Defense: Firearms

Including a firearm in your personal security plan is a serious decision that carries both tremendous responsibility and significant potential for lifesaving capability. Firearms offer an effective means of defense against lethal threats, but they also introduce *legal, ethical, and practical considerations* that must not be taken lightly. Before carrying or storing a firearm, it's critical to understand the laws in your jurisdiction regarding ownership, carry, storage, and use of force.

Equally important is a commitment to **regular, realistic training**—not just marksmanship, but safe handling, threat recognition, and decision-making under stress. You must also consider factors like safe storage in the home or vehicle, access by unauthorized individuals (especially children), and how a firearm fits into your daily lifestyle and environments.

A gun is not a magic solution—it's a tool that requires discipline, judgment, and preparation. If chosen, it should be integrated as a last resort into a broader personal security plan that emphasizes awareness, avoidance, and layered defense.

- **Handguns for Personal Protection:** If legally permitted, choose a reliable firearm suited to your ability to train and carry.

- **Concealed Carry Considerations:** Understand state laws, required permits, and proper holster selection.
- **Home Defense Firearms:** Handguns, shotguns, and carbines are common choices for home defense, but training and proper storage are essential considerations.
- **Training & Legal Knowledge:** Proficiency and understanding of self-defense laws are non-negotiable for responsible firearm ownership.

Final Thoughts

A personal security plan is not about living in fear—it's about being prepared. Whether at home, in your car, out in public, or at work, awareness and proactive measures reduce risk and enhance your ability to protect yourself and your loved ones. Security is a mindset, and the right preparation ensures that you can respond effectively should danger arise. In the next two chapters, we'll explore the basic categories of defensive firearms and non-lethal options, weighing the benefits and limitations of each.

CHAPTER 16

Choosing a Firearm for Self-Defense

Engaging in self-defense with a firearm is a profound responsibility that requires a clear understanding of both the capabilities and limitations of such weapons. Even among trained law enforcement officers, the realities of firearm use under extreme duress reveal significant challenges. This chapter explores these challenges and examines the suitability of the most common types of firearms—**pistols, revolvers, carbines, and shotguns**—for home defense scenarios.

Shooting Accuracy: A Sobering Reality

Law enforcement officers undergo extensive training to prepare for high-stress situations. The FBI has studied officer-involved shooting accuracy for decades to better understand performance under high-stress conditions. These studies consistently show that in real-world confrontations, typically occurring within 7 yards, officers often hit their intended target **less than 50%** of the time, with some studies showing accuracy rates **as low as 20–30%** during dynamic, rapidly evolving incidents.[10] Factors affecting accuracy include lighting, movement, stress response, suspect behavior, and the short time frame in which officers must assess threats and react.

These statistics underscore the inherent difficulties of accurate shooting under stress, where factors such as adrenaline, movement, and unpredictability of assailants come into play. The data highlights a critical difference between *static range* qualification and *actual gunfights*, underscoring the importance of scenario-based training, stress inoculation, and realistic force-on-force exercises to improve performance and reduce the risk of unintended harm.

---

[10]Michael D. White, "Hitting the Target (or Not): Comparing Characteristics of Fatal, Injurious, and Noninjurious Police Shootings," Police Quarterly 9, no. 3 (2006): 303, https://doi.org/10.1177/1098611105277199.

Simply put, hitting a moving, aggressive attacker while under extreme stress is *much harder* than most people imagine. For civilian defenders, this means that simply **owning a firearm is not enough**—training and practice are essential to developing real-world effectiveness.

Training unquestionably plays a critical role in developing proficiency, but the reality is that even the most experienced shooter is likely to **miss at least one** of the shots they fire in a dynamic, high-stress situation. That bullet is going to go into *something or someone* other than its intended target.

Unlike a law enforcement officer who may be protected by qualified immunity if they accidentally injure a bystander when using force, so-called "Good Samaritan" laws, designed to encourage people to help others in emergencies by shielding them from civil liability for providing reasonable assistance, **do not apply to civilians** who choose to intervene with a firearm. You *will* be held morally, civilly, and potentially criminally responsible for every round you fire, even in self-defense.

These realities aren't presented to dissuade you from incorporating a firearm into your personal security plans. Indeed, the firearm is the one tool that comes closest to leveling the playing field between assailant and defender, often playing the decisive role in determining the outcome of a violent conflict. The intent here is to ensure that you have the *facts* rather than the *fantasy* that Hollywood presents to help inform your decision-making when developing your personal security plan.

Firearms should be stored in a locked container that restricts unauthorized access - particularly from children - allowing access only to trained, responsible adults.

Pistols vs. Revolvers: Which is Right for You?

Photo by Delta Defense, LLC

Handguns are the most common choice for concealed carry and home defense due to their size, portability, and ease of storage. However, choosing between a **semi-automatic pistol** and a **revolver** is an important decision, as each type has distinct advantages and limitations.

Semi-Automatic Pistols

A semi-automatic pistol is the most popular defensive handgun choice today. These firearms use detachable magazines, allowing for faster reloading and higher ammunition capacity.

Advantages:

- **Higher Capacity** – Most modern pistols hold between 10-20 rounds, offering more chances to stop a threat before needing to reload.
- **Faster Reloads** – Magazines can be swapped out quickly, minimizing downtime in a firefight.
- **Lighter Trigger Pull** – Striker-fired pistols, such as the Glock 19 or SIG P320, typically have lighter and more consistent trigger pulls compared to revolvers.
- **Accessory Compatibility** – Many pistols have rails for mounting lights and optics, which can enhance effectiveness in defensive situations.

Limitations:

- **More Complex Operation** – Pistols require charging the weapon, or "racking the slide," clearing malfunctions, and understanding safeties, which may be difficult under stress.
- **Dexterity & Handstrength** – Some individuals may struggle with manipulating the slide and slide lock.
- **More Maintenance Required** – Semi-automatics generally require more cleaning and lubrication to ensure reliable function.
- **Ammunition Sensitivity** – Some pistols are prone to malfunctions with certain types of ammunition (a "failure to feed" the next round from the magazine).

Revolvers

Photo by Delta Defense, LLC

A revolver is a classic firearm known for its reliability and simplicity. These firearms operate with a rotating cylinder, typically holding 5 to 6 rounds.

Advantages:

- Extreme Reliability – With fewer moving parts, revolvers rarely experience malfunctions and can fire repeatedly even if the shooter has a weak grip.
- Simple Operation – No need to "rack a slide" or deal with magazines, simply pull the trigger to fire.

Limitations:

- Low Capacity – Most revolvers hold only 5-6 rounds, which may not be enough in a multiple-attacker situation.
- Slow Reloading – Reloading a revolver under stress is much slower than swapping a magazine in a pistol, even with speed loaders or moon clips.
- Heavy Trigger Pull – Double-action revolvers require 10-12 pounds of trigger pressure, which can affect accuracy, especially for shooters with less grip strength.
- Increased Recoil – Many revolvers lack the recoil mitigation of semi-autos, making follow-up shots more difficult.

Which is the Better Choice?

For *most* people, a semi-automatic pistol is the superior choice for self-defense due to its higher capacity, faster reloads, and ability to mount accessories. However, revolvers remain a solid option for those who prioritize simplicity and reliability over capacity.

Regardless of the choice, training and familiarity are crucial. A poorly trained shooter with a high-capacity pistol is far less effective than a well-trained shooter with a 5-shot revolver.

Carbines for Home Defense: Precision, Control, & Capacity

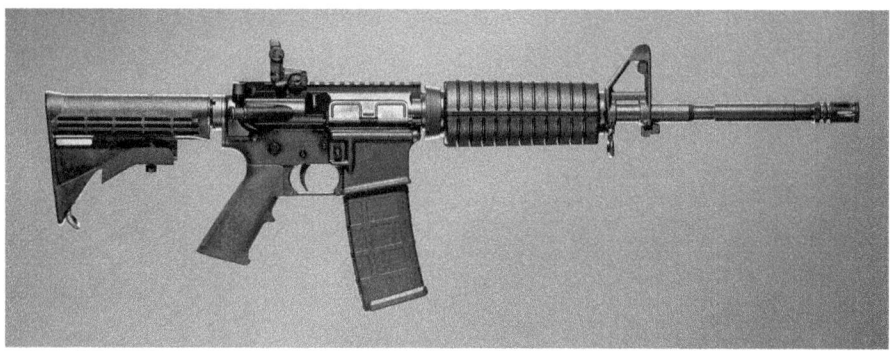

Carbines, particularly Colt-pattern carbines such as the AR-15, are rapidly growing in popularity and offer several advantages for home defense:

- **Increased Accuracy** – The shoulder-mounted design and longer sight radius drastically improve shooting precision, especially under stress.
- **Controlled Recoil** – Compared to handguns and shotguns, carbines typically produce less felt recoil, allowing for faster and more accurate follow-up shots.
- **Ammunition Capacity** – Most carbines have higher magazine capacities than shotguns or pistols, reducing the need for frequent reloading.
- **Ergonomic & Customizable** – Carbines allow for easy mounting of accessories such as lights, optics, and slings, which can enhance effectiveness in a defensive situation.

However, these benefits come with the *necessity for additional training*. While carbines are relatively easy to shoot, their manual of arms (reloading, malfunction clearing, and weapon manipulation) *requires a level of familiarity* that must be developed through consistent training.

Despite requiring some additional training, a properly configured carbine is one of the most effective defensive firearms available, offering superior accuracy, control, and firepower compared to a handgun.

Shotguns

Shotguns have long been a popular choice for home defense due to their so-called "stopping power" and versatility. However, understanding the **realities of shotgun effectiveness** is crucial before relying on one for personal protection.

Shotgun Ammunition Considerations

The effectiveness of a shotgun is *highly dependent* on the type of ammunition used:

- **Birdshot** – Usually containing hundreds of very tiny pellets (significantly limiting kinetic energy), this ammunition is *not ideal* for home defense.

- **Buckshot** – The preferred defensive load in many situations, offering a balance between spread and penetration. A *significant* consideration when considering buckshot is the necessity to account for all of the shot pellets.

  A typical 12-gauge 2 ¾ inch 00 buckshot shell holds 9 pellets—meaning that one trigger pull will send nine .33 caliber pellets down range simultaneously. This is highly effective at close range, especially if all 9 pellets hit the intended target. As with any round fired, those pellets that happen to miss are going to impact something or someone other than their intended target.

- **Rifled Slugs** – A one-ounce, .72 caliber piece of lead that provides devastating kinetic energy transfer and deep penetration, but *requires precise aiming* and poses risks of over-penetration.

Pump-Action vs. Semi-Automatic Shotguns

- **Pump-Action Shotguns** – Reliable but *require training* to cycle properly under stress.

- **Semi-Automatic Shotguns** – Faster follow-up shots, but require more maintenance and are more prone to malfunctions.

Shotguns can be effective, but they require *proper training* and careful ammunition selection to be suitable for home defense.

Final Thoughts

The decision to use a firearm for self-defense is complex and requires **realistic expectations** about performance under stress. FBI statistics on officer-involved shootings reveal that even highly trained individuals struggle significantly with accuracy in real-world engagements. This underscores the *absolute necessity* of training and regular practice for anyone choosing to own a firearm for defense.

- **Semi-automatic pistols** offer portability, higher capacity, and faster reloads, making them a solid choice for most people.

- **Revolvers** are simple and reliable, but their low capacity and slow reloads are significant drawbacks.

- **Colt-pattern carbines** provide greater accuracy, higher ammunition capacity, and lower recoil, making them one of the most effective home-defense weapons for those willing to train.

- **Shotguns** deliver significant "stopping power" at close range but require proper ammunition selection and training to be effective.

Regardless of the firearm you choose, training and preparation are key. Owning a firearm does not automatically make you safer—**the ability to use it effectively, under stress, is what matters.**

CHAPTER 17

Non-Lethal Self-Defense Weapons

While firearms remain the most effective tools for self-defense in life-threatening situations, they're not always the best or most appropriate option. Non-lethal self-defense weapons can provide an effective means of **stopping an attacker, deterring a threat, or creating an opportunity to escape**—without the legal, moral, and psychological implications of using deadly force.

This chapter explores the pros and cons of three popular non-lethal self-defense weapons: TASER energy weapons, pepper sprays, and non-lethal launchers. Understanding their strengths and limitations is critical for selecting the best option for your personal security plan.

TASER Energy Weapons

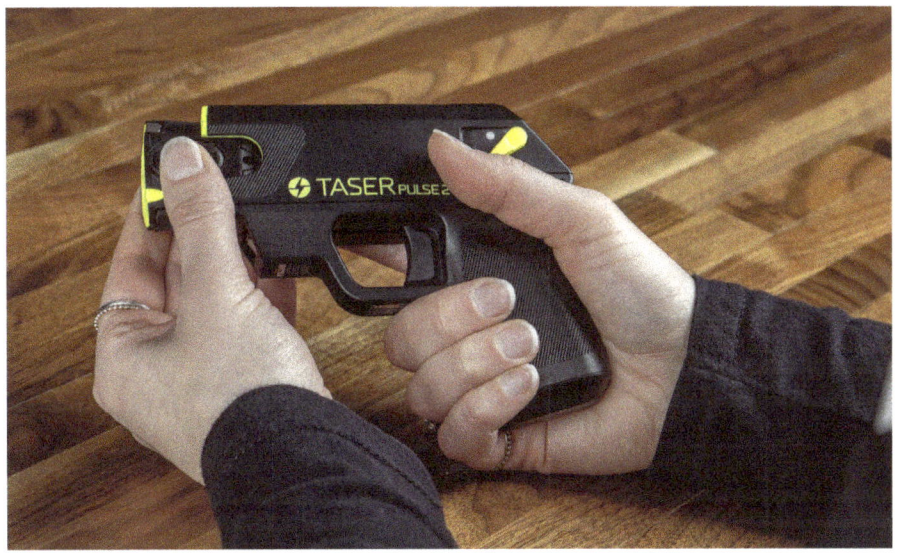

Photo by Delta Defense, LLC

TASER (an acronym which stands for Thomas **A.** Swift's Electric **Rifle**) energy weapons are electroshock devices that use **neuromuscular incapacitation (NMI)** to stop an attacker. Unlike stun guns, which require direct contact, TASERs fire two dart-like probes that deliver an electrical charge to the target from a distance, causing temporary paralysis and loss of motor control. It is critical to understand that *both darts must hit and penetrate* the attacker to complete the electric circuit to be effective.

TASER weapons are widely used by law enforcement and civilians alike as a non-lethal alternative to firearms.

Pros of TASERs

- **Effective at Stopping Threats** – A properly placed TASER shot can *completely incapacitate an attacker* (neuro-muscular incapacitation) for 5 to 30 seconds, depending on the model. This can provide a crucial window to escape.

- Axon, the company that manufactures TASER energy weapons, will **replace your weapon for free** if it's used and left behind (to allow you to escape) in a self-defense situation.

- **Can Be Used from a Distance** – Most civilian TASER models have an *effective range of 12-15 feet*, allowing the user to stop a threat before it reaches them.

- **Minimizes Legal and Moral Consequences** – TASERs are classified as non-lethal weapons, meaning they are generally seen as a *legally safer option* compared to firearms in self-defense situations.

- **Works on Drugged or Mentally Unstable Attackers** – Unlike pain-based deterrents (such as pepper spray), TASERs directly affect the nervous system, meaning they can *still be effective* against individuals under the influence of drugs or alcohol.

- **Built-In Safety Features** – Many civilian TASERs, such as the TASER Pulse, *include safety mechanisms* such as "Anti-Felon Identification" (AFID) tags that mark the scene of deployment and help prevent misuse.

Cons of TASERs

- **Limited Number of Shots** – Most civilian TASERs only carry one or two cartridges, meaning a miss or *multiple* attackers could leave the user defenseless.

- **Prone to Malfunctions** – If one probe misses or fails to penetrate clothing, the TASER *will not* work properly. The user must be prepared to transition to a backup self-defense method.

- **Shorter Range Compared to Firearms** – While TASERs allow for some standoff distance (up to 15 feet), this is *far less* than a firearm, meaning an attacker may still close the gap quickly.

- **Expensive to Own and Maintain** – TASER devices typically cost between $400 and $1,000, and replacement cartridges can be costly.

- **Restricted in Some Areas** – TASER laws vary by state and municipality, with some jurisdictions requiring permits or prohibiting civilian ownership altogether.

Pepper Spray

Pepper spray, also known as oleoresin capsicum (OC) spray, is a chemical irritant designed to cause intense pain, temporary blindness, and respiratory distress in attackers. It's widely used by law enforcement, civilians, and military personnel for self-defense and riot control.

Pepper sprays come in spray, gel, and foam formulations, with varying levels of intensity. Some are blended with **tear gas (CS gas) or UV dye** to enhance effectiveness and aid in suspect identification.

Stream and cone sprays are best used outdoors or at moderate distances of 6 to 12 feet. They provide either a wide coverage area or a focused stream, but can be affected by wind, risking self-exposure.

Gel formulations are ideal for indoor or confined spaces, sticking to an attacker's skin and eyes to prolong incapacitation. However, gels require more precise aiming due to their heavier consistency and narrower stream.

Foam formulations are effective indoors and for crowd control, expanding on contact to obscure an attacker's vision. They deliver irritants directly and cling to the face and eyes, but are most effective at close range within 6 to 8 feet.

Pros of Pepper Spray

- **Highly Portable** – Pepper spray is small, lightweight, and easy to carry, making it one of the most convenient self-defense options.

- **Works at a Distance** – Most pepper sprays have an effective range of 5-15 feet, allowing the user to engage threats *before* they get too close.

- **Incapacitating Effects** – Pepper spray causes temporary blindness, difficulty breathing, and intense pain, forcing attackers to stop and giving the user time to escape.

- **Multiple Uses per Canister** – Unlike a TASER, which only has one or two shots, pepper spray can be used multiple times per canister.

- **Affordable** – A high-quality pepper spray unit typically costs $10-$50, making it one of the most cost-effective self-defense tools.

- **Legal in Most Areas** – While some states restrict the size or concentration of pepper spray, it's legal in most locations and does not require a permit.

Cons of Pepper Spray

- **Requires Direct Contact to the Face** – Pepper spray is most effective when sprayed *directly* into an attacker's eyes and nose, which can be difficult under stress.

- **Wind and Blowback Risk** – If deployed in windy conditions, the spray may blow back into the user's face, causing self-contamination.

- **Does Not Work on Everyone** – Some attackers, especially those under the influence of drugs, alcohol, or extreme rage, *may* fight through the effects of pepper spray.

- **Can Take a Few Seconds to Work** – Unlike a TASER, which works instantly, pepper spray effects can take several seconds to incapacitate an attacker.

Non-Lethal Launchers

Photo by Delta Defense LLC

Non-lethal launchers are CO_2-powered weapons that fire kinetic and chemical projectiles. These launchers are gaining in popularity, especially among those who are looking for a viable, longer-range defensive weapon alternative to a firearm. These weapons **do not require a firearm license** and are marketed as a safe alternative to traditional firearms for self-defense.

These fire rounds that can deliver a painful kinetic impact or dispersible chemical irritants (pepper and tear gas compounds).

Pros of Non-Lethal Launchers

- Effective at a Longer Range – Launchers have a range of up to 60 feet, providing significantly greater standoff distance than a TASER or pepper spray.

- Multiple Shots Available – Most launchers hold 5-7 rounds per magazine, allowing for multiple engagements without reloading.

- Pain Compliance and Irritant Effects – Projectiles cause pain upon impact, and their chemical rounds create similar effects to pepper spray, enhancing their stopping power.

- No Recoil or Firearm-Like Operation – Launchers are easy to shoot, with no recoil and a simple point-and-shoot operation.

- Legal in Most Areas – Launchers are not classified as firearms and can be purchased without a background check in most states.

Cons of Non-Lethal Launchers

- **Less Immediate Stopping Power** – While painful, these projectiles are less *immediately incapacitating* than a TASER or firearm.

- **CO2 Dependent** – Launchers rely on CO_2 cartridges, which must be properly maintained and replaced over time.

- **Higher Cost Compared to Pepper Spray** – Launchers range from $300 to $500, making them a more significant investment.

Final Thoughts

Including non-lethal options in your personal security plan is essential for providing effective means of defense in non-permissive environments or in situations where the use of deadly force would be unnecessary, legally unjustified, or ethically inappropriate.

Each non-lethal weapon has **unique strengths and limitations**, and just like a firearm, none will be the perfect solution for every situation or environment. Ultimately, the best self-defense tool is *the one you are most comfortable carrying and using effectively.* Regular training and understanding the real-world limitations of any self-defense weapon are critical to ensuring it serves its intended purpose—**keeping you safe.**

CHAPTER 18

When the Police Arrive

Navigating the Most Dangerous Phase

A self-defense incident doesn't end when the immediate threat is neutralized. In many ways, the moments after a violent encounter can be just as dangerous—both physically and legally. It's important to keep in mind that even if it wasn't an "armed conflict" before the police were called, it certainly becomes one when they arrive.

Law enforcement officers are always armed, and they don't know who the "good guy" is right away. The first few moments after the police arrive are fraught with peril, with a very real likelihood of misunderstanding due to the initial chaos. Knowing how to interact with law enforcement in these situations *can be the difference between walking away and facing unintended consequences.*

This chapter will guide you through what to expect when the police arrive after a self-defense incident, how to protect yourself legally, and best practices for any interaction with law enforcement—including traffic stops. We'll also address your rights, including **the Fifth Amendment's protection** against self-incrimination, and the best approach to communicating (or not communicating) after a critical event.

What to Expect When Law Enforcement Arrives After a Self-Defense Incident

Photo by Delta Defense, LLC

The moments after a self-defense incident are some of the most dangerous and critical you will ever face. Even if you were completely justified in your actions, law enforcement officers arriving at the scene do not know what transpired. **Their primary objective** is to secure the scene, assess potential threats, and restore order. Knowing how to conduct yourself when police arrive can mean the difference between walking away or being arrested … or potentially far worse.

If the attacker is down or has fled and no longer poses an imminent threat, **do not continue using force**. If practical, improve your position by moving to a safer location, especially if you're in a public place. For example, if you were attacked at a gas station, you may consider moving inside to await law enforcement's arrival. If safe to do so, holster or place your firearm on the ground or away from your body before police arrive to avoid appearing as a potential threat to their safety.

When the police arrive at the scene, *they don't know* who the aggressor is. Here's what you should expect:

1. **Officers Will Be on High Alert** – They will arrive expecting danger. Even if you're the victim, they may treat you as a potential suspect until they can assess the situation. *Don't make sudden movements*, and follow all commands.

2. **You Will Likely Be Ordered to the Ground or Handcuffed** – This is standard procedure. Being handcuffed does *not* mean you are guilty. It's a temporary measure for officer safety. Do not resist.

3. **They Will Secure Any Weapons** – If you have a firearm or other weapon, the officers will take control of it. Keep your hands visible, and do not reach for anything unless instructed.

4. **You Will Be Questioned** – Officers will ask you what happened. *Your response is critical*—and saying too much could lead to self-incrimination.

What to Say (and Not Say) After a Self-Defense Incident

Many legal experts recommend following a *minimalist* approach when speaking to law enforcement after a self-defense incident.

Here's what you should say:

1. **"Officer, I was attacked."**
2. **"I was in fear for my life."**
3. **"I want to press charges."**
4. **"Here is the evidence."** Point out any weapons the attacker used, security cameras, or witnesses.
5. **"I will fully cooperate after speaking with my attorney."**

Beyond this, do not say anything else. The stress and adrenaline of the situation may cause you to say things that can be misinterpreted or used against you later. Even innocent statements can be taken out of context or twisted in a legal setting.

Why You Should Wait for an Attorney

Your memory immediately after a high-stress event is unreliable. You may say something inaccurate without realizing it, and that statement will be recorded and possibly used against you. An attorney will help you provide an accurate statement **after you've had time to calm down.**

<u>Understanding the Miranda Warning and the Right to Remain Silent</u>

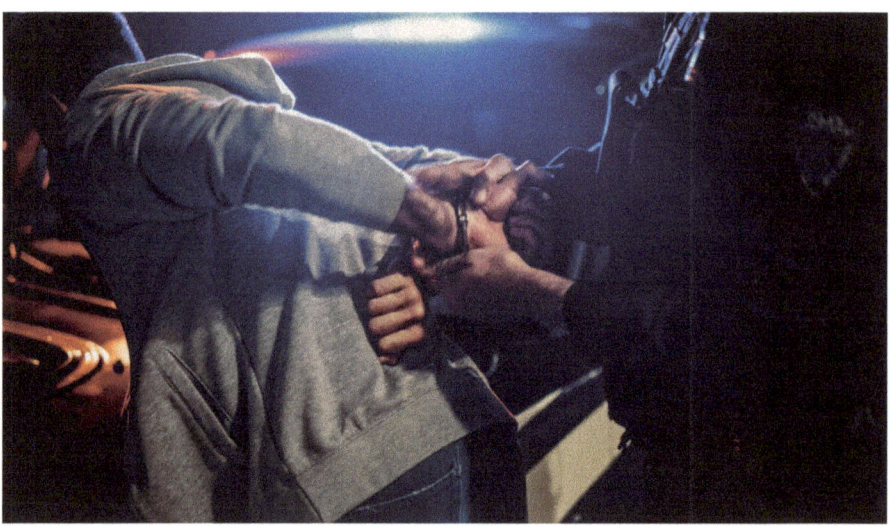

Understanding your legal rights when interacting with law enforcement is crucial to protecting yourself in any situation. The difference between **being detained and being taken into custody** by law enforcement lies in the level of restriction on a person's freedom and the legal implications of each situation.

During an investigative detention—also known as a Terry stop—law enforcement may temporarily detain you if they have **reasonable suspicion** that you're involved in criminal activity. This is not the same as an arrest, but *you are not free to leave* during the stop. Even while detained, you retain key constitutional rights:

Under the **Fourth Amendment**, you are protected from unreasonable searches and seizures, meaning officers must have reasonable suspicion to detain you and may only frisk you for weapons if they believe you are armed and dangerous.

Under the **Fifth Amendment**, you have the right to remain silent; you are *not required to answer questions beyond identifying yourself* if state law requires it.

While a detention can lead to an arrest if officers gather enough evidence (from having a *reasonable suspicion* that the individual may have committed a crime to having *probable cause* to believe so), not all detentions result in someone being taken into custody.

Under the **Sixth Amendment**, if the detention escalates into an arrest, you have the right to an attorney. It's important to remain calm, ask if you're free to go, and clearly state that you wish to remain silent and speak to a lawyer if questioned further.

In order to affirm and exercise these rights, you should clearly state, "I'm invoking my right to remain silent and would like to speak to a lawyer." It's important to remember that anything you say **can and will be used against you** in court, so staying silent until legal counsel is present is often the safest course of action.

What the Miranda Warning Means

As described above, law enforcement has the right to detain you temporarily, *without* advising you of your "Miranda" rights. However, if you're taken into custody (under arrest), law enforcement **must inform** you of your rights:

- You have the right to remain silent.
- Anything you say can and will be used against you in a court of law.
- You have the right to an attorney.
- If you cannot afford an attorney, one will be appointed to you.

Social Pressure to Talk & How to Resist It

Many people feel compelled to justify their actions when interacting with police. This is a *mistake* in self-defense incidents.

Why People Feel Pressured to Talk

- **Natural Human Reaction:** We want to explain ourselves to avoid seeming guilty.
- **Police Officers Seem Friendly:** Many officers use a conversational tone to extract statements.
- **Innocent People Think the Truth Will Set Them Free:** Unfortunately, statements made in distress can be misinterpreted or used against you.

How to Resist the Pressure

- **Repeat Your Prepared Statement**
  "I will cooperate after speaking to my attorney."

- **Politely Decline to Answer More Questions**
  "I understand, but I would like legal counsel present."

- **Recognize That Silence Is Not Guilt**
  it is *wisdom* and it is your constitutionally guaranteed *right*.

Best Practices for Any Law Enforcement Interaction

Whether during a self-defense incident, a traffic stop, or any other encounter, knowing how to interact with police is essential. Here's how to handle these situations professionally and safely:

During a Traffic Stop

If pulled over by police, follow these steps:

1. **Pull Over Safely:**

   Find a well-lit area, preferably one with plenty of room for the officer to approach your vehicle on foot. Slow down and use your turn signal to indicate to the officer that you are acknowledging his direction to stop, and pull over smoothly.

   Put the car in park.
   If at night, turn on the interior cabin light.
   Roll down your windows to allow the officer to see inside your vehicle as they approach.
   Turn off the radio.
   Turn off the engine.

2. **Stay Calm and Keep Your Hands Visible**:

Keep your hands on top of the steering wheel, with the tips of your thumbs touching and your fingers spread.

Don't reach for anything until directed to do so.

3. **Be Polite and Respectful**:

Avoid aggressive or confrontational behavior. Address the officer
as "Sir" or "Ma'am" and follow instructions.

4. **Know Your Rights**:

You *must* provide your driver's license, registration, and proof of insurance.

You do not have to consent to a vehicle search unless the officer has **probable cause** to believe that evidence of a crime is inside. This is *not for you to decide* or debate here. If the officer insists on searching your vehicle, you should clearly state that you are not giving your consent to the search, and then get out of the way. Whether or not that search was indeed lawful (and thus if any evidence recovered as a result of that search is admissible) will be determined by the court.

You have the right to **remain silent**—politely decline to answer questions unrelated to the stop.

Should You Tell the Officer You Have a Firearm?

Laws vary by state regarding whether you must inform an officer that you have a concealed carry permit or firearm in your vehicle. However, general best practices include:

- If required by law in your state, *immediately inform the officer* that you are a concealed carrier and have a firearm.
- If not required, you may choose not to disclose unless asked. However, if the officer *asks directly*, always answer truthfully.

- **Never reach for the weapon**. If asked for your ID, calmly say, "Officer, my ID is in my wallet, and my firearm is in the glove box. How would you like me to proceed?"

DO <u>NOT</u> say:

- "I have a gun!" This could be misinterpreted as a threat.

What if you're stopped on foot?

- Keep your hands visible.
- Don't make sudden movements.
- If questioned, politely ask, "**Am I being detained, or am I free to go?**" If you are not being detained, you can walk away.
- If detained, you do <u>not</u> have to answer questions beyond providing identification if required by law.

Surviving the Most Dangerous Phase

The moment the police arrive is often unpredictable and chaotic. Officers don't know the full story, and miscommunication can be deadly. To ensure your safety:

- **Do not argue or resist.** Even if you feel wronged, comply and deal with legal issues later, in the safety of the police station or courtroom—*with your attorney.*
- **Keep your hands visible at all times.** If the police can see your hands are empty, they're less likely to perceive you as an immediate threat.
- **Move slowly and follow commands exactly.** No sudden movements.
- **Be mindful of body language and tone.** Officers are trained to detect aggression, resistance, or deception.

Final Thoughts

Understanding how to interact with law enforcement—whether after a self-defense incident, during a traffic stop, or any other encounter—is crucial for your safety and legal protection.

The **right to remain silent** is one of the most powerful legal protections you have, and the right to an attorney is non-negotiable. By understanding your rights and best practices for handling law enforcement interactions, you can protect yourself *both physically and legally* in any situation.

If involved in a self-defense incident:

1. **Call 911** and request both police and medical assistance.
2. **Say only what's necessary,** "I was attacked. I was in fear for my life. I want to press charges. I will cooperate after speaking with my attorney." Do not provide excessive details over the phone; the call is recorded even before the call taker connects.
3. **Don't attempt to justify or explain.** This is not the time to defend your actions.
4. **Do not answer further questions** until your lawyer is present.

The moments following a self-defense incident are critical, and how you handle interactions with law enforcement can shape the outcome. Always remember:

- Police arriving on the scene **don't know** who the good guy is, don't make yourself appear as a threat.
- **Don't make statements** beyond reporting that you were attacked and will cooperate *after* speaking with an attorney.
- Know your rights, invoke your **right to remain silent** and request **legal representation.**
- In all police interactions, stay calm, be respectful, and **do not waive** your legal protections.

By understanding the dynamics of police encounters and preparing in advance, you can ensure that you protect yourself— not just in the moment of self-defense, but also in the legal and social aftermath.

CHAPTER 19

Lifesaving in the Aftermath: Trauma Care After a Self-Defense Situation

After a self-defense incident, someone—maybe even you—might be injured. Whether it was defending your home, protecting your loved ones, or responding to a violent threat, the danger has now passed, but what happens next is **just as critical.**

Help may still be minutes or more away. In those precious moments before first responders arrive, the ability to provide immediate trauma care can make the difference between life and death. The good news: *You don't need to be a medic to save a life.*

Your Role: Life Preserver

Violent encounters often lead to serious injuries—gunshot wounds, stab wounds, broken bones, and heavy bleeding. These injuries can be fatal in minutes if not addressed quickly. But the reality is, when the dust settles after a self-defense event, you may be the only one in a position to help until EMS gets there. Remember, the mission here is not to "fix" or "repair" what is wrong; it's simply to **buy time** to get to someone (usually a surgeon at a hospital) who can.

You don't need a medical degree. You just need a calm mindset, the willingness to act, and a *basic understanding* of how to keep someone alive.

Massive blood loss rapidly reduces **perfusion**, the delivery of oxygen-rich blood to vital organs like the brain, heart, and kidneys. Without adequate perfusion, these organs begin to shut down within minutes. Stopping bleeding is the fastest way to maintain circulation and give the body a fighting chance to survive until help arrives. *You are literally buying time for the brain and heart to stay alive.*

That's where the **MARCH** mnemonic comes in—a simple system designed for battlefield medics, now widely used by first responders and even civilians across the country.

The MARCH Mnemonic for First Responders

MARCH helps you *prioritize* care in the *correct order* when someone is badly hurt. It's important to remember that you don't move on to the next "letter" until you are satisfied that you have adequately addressed the current one. It makes no sense to address "Hypothermia" if an unaddressed **M**assive hemorrhage is spilling that blood onto the ground where it cannot perfuse vital organs, you are trying to keep alive!

M.A.R.C.H. stands for:

1. **M** – Massive Hemorrhage
2. **A** – Airway
3. **R** – Respiration
4. **C** – Circulation
5. **H** – Head Injury / Hypothermia

Let's break it down.

 **M – Massive Hemorrhage**

First priority: Stop the bleeding. Gunshots, knife wounds, and broken glass can cause catastrophic bleeding that kills within minutes.

What you can do:

- Look for pooling blood, soaked clothing, or visible wounds.

- Apply firm, **direct pressure directly on the wound** with a cloth, a shirt, or even your hand. The goal here is to crimp the flow of blood out of the wound. Think of your arteries as a garden hose. If you cut a hose, water begins to jet out. By "crimping" or compressing that hose, you may not stop the flow completely, but you will significantly reduce the amount of water (blood) lost, which *buys time.*

- If you have a tourniquet (or an improvised one), use it for bleeding on arms or legs. Place the tourniquet high up on the arm or leg, just below the junction with the shoulder or hip. The large bone beneath (humerus/femur) provides an excellent place to squeeze against—**tighten the tourniquet until bleeding stops.** If possible, write the time the tourniquet was placed on the patient so the hospital knows how long it's been applied.

- If the wound is deep and bleeding heavily, pack it with clean cloth or gauze and press hard. Wound "packing" is for extremity (arms/legs) or junctional (where the arms or legs meet the body) wounds only.

  NEVER pack a head, neck, chest, or abdominal wound!
  Use a surface/pressure bandages only on wounds to these areas.

Pro Tip: Keep a trauma kit in your home or vehicle with a tourniquet, gauze, and gloves. It's the fire extinguisher of medical emergencies—it's far better to have it and not need it than to need it and not have it.

A – Airway

Next: Make sure the person can breathe. If someone is unconscious or has facial injuries, their airway might be blocked.

What you can do:

- Talk to the person. If they respond, their airway is open.
- If they're unresponsive and not breathing properly, gently tilt their head back and lift the chin to open the airway.

- Remove any visible obstructions like blood, vomit, or debris if you can safely do so.
- If they are breathing but unconscious, roll them on their side into the "recovery position."

ProTip: In unconscious people, *the tongue is the most common cause* of airway blockage. When someone loses muscle tone, the tongue can relax and fall back into the throat, blocking airflow. Tilting the head back and lifting the chin can lift the tongue away from the airway and restore breathing. This simple action can be lifesaving, especially when no equipment is available.

The "recovery position" uses gravity to help pull the tongue away from the back of the throat (this is the same reason your spouse may elbow you to roll onto your side if you're snoring). This also helps mitigate the chance of choking on vomit.

 **R – Respiration**

Now, check for chest injuries. A puncture to the chest—especially from a bullet or knife—can collapse a lung or allow air to enter the chest cavity, causing deadly internal pressure buildup.

What you can do:

- Expose the chest and look for entry/exit wounds. Check front and back - if there is an entry wound, there may be a corresponding exit wound.
- If you see a hole in the chest, cover it with an airtight seal (like plastic wrap, a sandwich bag, or a rubber glove) taped on three sides. This lets air out but not in.
- Keep the person calm and sitting slightly upright if they're having trouble breathing.

When and how to give rescue breaths without CPR:

If the person has a pulse, but isn't breathing, start rescue breathing *only*.

- 1 breath every 5–6 seconds (about 10–12 breaths per minute).
- Watch for chest rise with each breath. This technique helps main-

tain oxygenation and is useful *when the heart is still working* but breathing has stopped.

- Recheck pulse and breathing every 2 minutes. If the pulse stops, **then begin full CPR immediately:**

When and how to give rescue breaths <u>during</u> CPR:

If you have a barrier device (or feel comfortable doing so without one), give **2 breaths after every 30 compressions.** Tilt the head back, pinch the nose, and give a breath over 1 second—just enough to see the chest rise.

If you don't have help, you can focus on **hands-only CPR**: no breaths, just compressions. The oxygen in the bloodstream is usually enough to maintain minimal perfusion for a short time. Keep going until EMS takes over or the person shows signs of life.

 C – Circulation

Even if you've stopped the bleeding, the body might still be going into shock. Shock is the body's autonomic response to not getting enough blood flow to vital organs. In the **early stages of shock**, the body is still fighting to maintain blood pressure and organ function.

Signs include fast breathing, rapid heart rate, pale or cool skin, and anxiety. In the late stages of shock, blood pressure crashes, and organs begin to fail due to a lack of perfusion.

What you can do:

- Keep the person lying flat unless they're struggling to breathe.
- Elevate their legs if there are no obvious injuries to them.
- Keep them calm and still.
- Do not give them anything to eat or drink, even if they ask.
  When to perform CPR:

If a person is **unconscious, not breathing, and has no pulse, begin CPR (cardiopulmonary resuscitation)** immediately. This means 100–120 chest compressions per minute, at least 2 inches deep in the center of the chest (roughly the same cadence as Staying Alive by the Bee Gees). The goal is to manually pump blood to keep the brain and heart alive until help arrives. Keep going until EMS takes over or the person starts breathing again.

H – Head Injury / Hypothermia

Finally, consider the head and the risk of hypothermia, even if it's warm out. Blood loss can lower body temperature fast, which worsens shock.

What you can do:

- Watch for confusion, unconsciousness, or unequal pupils—these can be signs of a head injury.
- Never "pack" a head wound! Cover any bleeding wounds with a pressure bandage.
- Keep the person warm. Use a jacket, blanket, or even
- your body heat.
- Avoid moving them unless absolutely necessary, especially if they've hit their head or fallen.

Next Steps: Why Warmth Matters

Trauma victims lose body heat fast—even in warm weather. Cold blood doesn't clot well, and hypothermia worsens shock. **Always keep the patient warm** with blankets, coats, or whatever is available.

Cover the ground beneath them or move them onto something that will insulate them from the ground if possible. Even on a relatively warm concrete floor, the laws of thermodynamics apply: If it's cooler than 98.6 degrees, that concrete will draw the heat away from the body until it is the same temperature as the concrete.

Is "Defund" Affecting EMS Response Times?

The "defund" movement has ramifications well beyond law enforcement response times. In any situation, emergency medical first responders are trained to determine "Is the scene safe?" prior to going in to try and render aid. In a violence-related emergency (reports of "shots fired", etc), most fire departments or ambulance services have a rule in place requiring them to "stage" or wait nearby (usually a mile or more away) until law enforcement has arrived.

Only after the situation has been assessed and law enforcement has given the "all clear," will these unarmed/unarmored medical responders come to the scene to render aid to the victims; otherwise, they run the very real risk of becoming victims themselves.

As a SWAT operator for the FBI, I was also an Emergency Medical Technician (EMT) and served as the lead medic for my team. To keep our certifications current, SWAT medics would occasionally "ride along" with a local ambulance crew.

One such evening in 2015 (*long before* the "defund" movement) served to open my eyes to how dire the situation is in many areas. This typical Tuesday evening in downtown Detroit, I rode along with an ambulance crew of two EMTs, both of whom had been on the job for several years.

Our very first call for service was a report of a shooting only a few miles from the station. When we were about a mile from the scene, the driver pulled into a deserted parking lot and parked. I couldn't understand what we were doing, but as a "guest," I didn't want to question why we weren't rushing to help.

After about 15 minutes of idling in the parking lot, the driver turned around and headed back towards the station, never even glimpsing the scene! I finally asked why we weren't going to try and help, and the driver explained that the police had not arrived yet. **Without police presence to stabilize the situation**, it was understandably against fire department policy to send in these unarmed responders.

These EMTs explained that, due to the length of time it took for law enforcement, and therefore medical help to arrive, it was almost certain that the victim or victims had either self-transported to a hospital or were already dead at the scene. This same scenario replayed itself three more times that evening. I was assured that this was absolutely routine and that, *more times than not*, their ambulance never even arrived at the scene of a reported shooting.

This scenario is being played out every single day in cities and communities all over America.

Should I Provide Aid to My Attacker?

In the aftermath of a defensive encounter, the question of whether to render medical aid to an attacker who has been incapacitated is complex and must be approached with extreme caution.

While a moral or ethical inclination to provide aid may exist, your primary responsibility is to ensure your own safety and the safety of those around you. An attacker **may still pose a threat**, feign incapacitation, or have concealed weapons, making any approach potentially dangerous.

Legally, civilians are generally *under no obligation* to render aid in such situations, especially if doing so places them at risk. The best course of action is to secure the scene, contact emergency services immediately, and provide them with clear information.

If you're in a position to safely monitor the assailant's condition from a distance while waiting for first responders, that may be appropriate—but **physically intervening is rarely advisable** unless you're trained and *certain* the threat has been neutralized. Always defer to local laws and your training when making such decisions.

Final Thoughts

When violence occurs, EMS will come, eventually, but YOU are the first responder. In the wake of a self-defense situation, whether someone else was injured or you were hurt yourself, taking action while waiting for help can save a life—*maybe your own*.

The **MARCH method** gives you structure in chaos. You don't need to remember every medical term, just this order: Control bleeding, check the airway, support breathing, monitor circulation, and guard against head injury and cold (hypothermia).

After defending yourself, your survival mindset doesn't end—*it shifts*. The danger from an attacker may have passed, but someone's life could still hang in the balance. Knowing what to do *and doing it* can make the difference between tragedy and survival.

CHAPTER 20

The Legal Aftermath

Addressing the Gap in Most Security Plans

When most people design a personal security plan, they focus on **prevention and physical protection:** secure doors, situational awareness, training with defensive tools, and emergency response plans.

These are essential pillars, but there's a common blind spot in many well-intentioned strategies: **the legal aftermath.** Surviving a violent encounter is only the beginning. What comes next can be financially and emotionally devastating, even if you did *everything* right.

When building a holistic personal security plan, it's essential to consider not just how you defend yourself, but also what happens *after* a self-defense incident. It's easy to assume that if you're in the right and act lawfully, the situation ends when the threat is stopped. Unfortunately, that's not always the case.

Even if your actions are legally justified, you could still face criminal charges, civil lawsuits, or significant legal fees. That's where **self-defense liability insurance** becomes a critical part of your personal security strategy.

This type of coverage provides financial and legal support in the aftermath of a defensive use of force, including attorney fees, bail coverage, expert witnesses, and civil defense costs.

Just like carrying a firearm or other defensive tool, having a plan for legal protection is part of being fully prepared. It ensures that a single moment of survival doesn't turn into years of financial or legal devastation—and allows you to focus on recovery, not ruin.

The Hidden Cost of a Self-Defense Incident

In the real world, the aftermath of a defensive encounter can be legally and financially devastating. You could be detained, arrested, charged, or sued by the attacker or their family. Your firearm could be taken as evidence, and your home or property might be part of an active investigation. Legal battles can take months or even years to resolve, and **attorney fees alone can easily exceed $30,000–$200,000**, depending on the case.

And if you're sued in civil court, you're on your own unless you have legal coverage. You could face months or *years* of legal battles and mounting costs.

Why Self-Defense Liability Insurance Matters

Self-defense liability insurance—also referred to as concealed carry insurance or a legal protection membership—provides the legal and financial support you may desperately need following a use-of-force incident. Reputable self-defense insurance or legal insurance memberships typically offer:

- Coverage for **criminal defense** legal fees
- Coverage for **civil defense** legal fees
- **Civil liability** coverage

- **Bail bond** funding
- Expert **witness fees**
- **Lost wages** during legal proceedings
- Firearm or tool **replacement**

Some providers also offer **24/7 emergency hotlines** to help you navigate the chaos and match you with an experienced attorney immediately after an incident—*before* giving a formal statement to police.

You Don't Have to Be a Firearm Carrier

Contrary to popular belief, self-defense liability insurance isn't just for those who own or carry firearms. Anyone who might use a weapon, tool, or even their bare hands in self-defense can benefit from it.

Knife owners, martial artists, or even individuals who keep a baseball bat by the door for home protection could face legal consequences for using force—*even if it's justified*. The legal system doesn't always move quickly, and the truth about what happened isn't always obvious to investigators. Having coverage ensures that your rights are defended while the system sorts out the facts.

Legal Justification Does NOT Guarantee Legal Protection

One of the most common misconceptions is that if you acted within the law, you have nothing to worry about.

While that should be true in theory, in practice, the criminal justice system is complex and varies greatly depending on jurisdiction, public perception, and even political pressure. Prosecutors may still bring charges, especially if the incident draws media attention or involves the use of deadly force. **Civil lawsuits**, where the burden of proof is much lower, can be filed *even if you're acquitted criminally.*

Insurance or legal protection ensures you're not left to navigate this alone or forced to choose between defending yourself in court and protecting your financial future.

Choosing the Right Coverage

There are several reputable providers of self-defense liability insurance and legal protection plans. When comparing them, consider:

- Is coverage available in your state?
- What's the cap on civil or criminal defense?
- What's the limit on civil damages or legal costs?
- Can I choose my own attorney?
- Is bail covered up front or reimbursed later? And if so, how much?
- Are incidents involving non-firearms (hands, knives, less-lethal tools) included?
- Do they cover appeals, expert witnesses, and court costs?
- Are appeals and retrials included?

Just like any insurance, the best time to get it is *before* you need it. The aftermath of an incident is, unfortunately, too late to realize you should have purchased a plan.

I personally recommend looking for a solution that's MORE than just an insurance policy. Products like USCCA Membership include self-defense education materials, legal resources, and lifesaving training, along with a robust policy in their member benefits.

While SDLI is, in my opinion, essential in this day and age—the training to know how to respond to trouble or stay *out* of it altogether—is just as critical.

Peace of Mind Is Part of the Plan

Photo by Delta Defense, LLC

Having legal protection in place offers financial security and peace of mind —*after a defensive incident*. It means you can focus on doing what's necessary to stay safe, knowing that if the worst happens, you won't be alone in dealing with the aftermath. It also helps protect your family from the financial and emotional burden that the legal fallout can bring.

Preparedness doesn't end when the threat is over. In fact, your responsibilities may have only just begun. A holistic personal security plan covers the **before**, the **during**, and the **after** of any defensive scenario. Self-defense liability insurance is the *critical bridge* between the legal system and your ability to move forward with your life.

Key Takeaways:

- Even justified self-defense can lead to arrest, charges, or lawsuits.
- Legal costs can easily exceed **$30,000–$100,000** or more.
- Insurance or legal membership plans cover attorneys, bail, damages, and more.
- It's valuable even if you never carry a gun.
- Legal preparedness is part of being truly secure.

Final Thoughts

Self-defense insurance isn't just for those who carry a firearm. Even justified self-defense can lead to arrest, prosecution, or civil litigation. If you use *any* force—your hands, a blunt object, a knife, or even a less-lethal option like pepper spray—you may face legal scrutiny.

Just because a use of force is justified, that *doesn't mean you'll be protected* by the legal system. Insurance ensures you're not left alone to defend yourself legally after defending yourself physically.

Being prepared doesn't end when the threat is neutralized. A truly comprehensive security mindset addresses what happens **before, during, and after** a defensive encounter.

Self-defense liability insurance bridges the critical gap between physical safety and long-term protection and is a core element of a complete personal security plan. It allows you to make responsible, lifesaving decisions in the moment without fearing financial ruin in the aftermath.

CHAPTER 21

Your Personal Security Journey

Throughout this book, we've explored the essential elements of personal security—not just as a set of tools or tactics, but as a mindset, a discipline, and a lifestyle. By becoming more proactive, informed, and intentional, you've taken meaningful steps toward becoming a competent and confident stakeholder in your own safety and security.

What You've Learned

From understanding situational awareness and risk assessment to setting up secure environments and responding to emergencies, you've built a strong foundation:

- **Mindset & Awareness:** You learned to trust your instincts, recognize red flags, and stay alert without becoming paranoid.
- **Preparation & Planning:** You now know how to assess threats, make contingency plans, and protect your physical spaces.
- **Practical Skills:** Whether it's creating a go-bag, learning self-defense principles, or setting boundaries, you have practical, actionable tools to apply.

Moving Forward

Security is not a destination; it's a **continuous process**. Threats evolve, environments change, and new tools emerge. The goal is not to live in fear, but to live with confidence—knowing you have the mindset, skills, and plans to handle uncertainty.

Here's how to keep progressing:

- **Stay Current:** Regularly review your plans, tools, and habits. Follow credible sources on safety and security.
- **Train & Practice:** Run drills, update your skills, and stay physically and mentally prepared.
- **Share & Empower:** Help others become more aware and capable. Empower your family, friends, and colleagues.
- **Stay Grounded:** Keep security in perspective. The objective is to enhance your quality of life, not limit it.

Final Thoughts

Your personal security is ultimately your responsibility, but you are not alone. By choosing to engage with the principles in this guide, you've already done more than most, equipping yourself not just with knowledge but with the confidence and competence to act decisively. Security is not about fear. It's about **freedom**—the freedom to move through the world with awareness, resilience, and peace of mind.

APPENDIX

The Checklists

Action Items for Your Personal Security Journey

Preparation is *essential* to ensuring the highest probability of securing a positive outcome during a critical event. A checklist is a form of "**Premade Decisions**" discussed earlier.

Significant peace of mind comes with the confidence of knowing that you're prepared—with both the physical tools and the mental commitment—to respond effectively should the unexpected arise.

The following checklists are provided to help you organize, categorize, and prioritize the many decisions along *your* **Personal Security Journey**.

In those cases where a specific provider or company is named, I have personally verified the quality and efficacy of that product, but do not benefit financially from this endorsement.

CHECKLIST:
Upgrading the Physical Security of Your Home

Exterior Doors

- Replace hollow-core doors with solid wood, steel, or fiberglass alternatives.
- Install a **reinforced strike plate** with 3" screws penetrating deep into the frame.
- Use **deadbolt locks** with a minimum 1" throw.
- Add **door reinforcement hardware**, such as door jammers or security bars.
- Use **smart locks** or high-security keyed systems with restricted duplication.
- Install a **peephole or door viewer** with a wide-angle lens.

Windows

- Use **window locks** on all ground-level and basement windows.
- Add **window security film** to resist shattering.
- Install **window sensors** for alarms or smart home integration.
- Reinforce accessible windows with **security bars or grilles** (especially basement windows).
- Plant **thorny shrubs** or bushes beneath accessible windows for natural deterrence.

Alarm & Surveillance Systems

- Install a monitored alarm system covering doors, windows, and motion zones.
- Place visible security cameras at all entry points and perimeter zones.
- Ensure video doorbells are installed and connected to cloud storage.
- Add motion-activated lights near all entrances and along walkways.
- Ensure backup power for alarms and cameras in case of outages.

Outdoor & Perimeter Security

- Keep landscaping trimmed to eliminate hiding places near doors and windows.
- Install fencing with locking gates to control access to the yard.
- Secure outdoor sheds and garages with strong locks and alarm sensors.
- Store ladders and tools inside to prevent intruder access.

Garage Security

- Install **deadbolts** or high-security locks on doors between the garage and the home.
- Disable or secure **emergency release levers** on automatic garage doors.
- Keep garage doors closed and locked at all times, even when at home.
- Add **motion sensor lighting** in and around the garage.

Interior Layers of Security

- Pre-position barricade devices in bedrooms and other logical rooms. (eg. MasterLock Security Door Bar)
- Designate and secure a **safe room** or reinforced area for emergencies.
- Secure valuables in a **heavy, bolted-down safe** with fire and theft protection.
- Use **curtains or frosted film** on windows to block the view into the home.

Habits & Awareness

- **Lock** all doors and windows, even when at home.
- Don't leave **spare keys** in obvious places (e.g., under the doormat or flowerpots).
- Vary your **daily routines** to avoid patterns.
  Train family members on **emergency procedures** and safe zones.
- **Regularly test** your alarm and camera systems.

CHECKLIST:
Developing a Family Emergency & Reunification Plan

Emergencies can happen quickly and without warning. A well-thought-out plan helps ensure your family knows **how to communicate, where to go, and what to do** in the event of a disaster, evacuation, or other crisis. This checklist will help you build a solid foundation for preparedness and peace of mind.

Step 1: Establish Emergency Communication Protocols

- Identify a **primary point of contact** outside your region (e.g., a relative in another state).
- Choose at least **two communication methods** (text, call, radio app, group chat).
- Designate a **group chat or emergency alert channel** (e.g., Signal, WhatsApp).
- Teach children how to use cell phones or radios to reach parents or guardians.
- Keep a **paper list of key contacts** in wallets, backpacks, and go-bags. Consider laminating this card for durability.

Step 2: Define Emergency Meeting Points

- Set a **primary meeting place near the home** (e.g., neighbor's porch, mailbox).
- Designate a **secondary local meeting place** in case the neighborhood is inaccessible (e.g., library, school, place of worship).
- Choose a **regional meeting location** (e.g., relative's house or town hall) for wide-area emergencies.
- Ensure **everyone knows how to get to each location** on foot, by vehicle, or by public transit.

Step 3: Identify Types of Emergencies & Response Plans

- Create **tailored plans** for various scenarios:
    - Fire
    - Natural disaster (flood, earthquake, tornado, etc.)
    - Home invasion
    - Civil unrest or lockdown
    - Missing person/kidnapping
- Teach all family members the **appropriate response** actions for each scenario.
- Rehearse **fire drills and shelter-in-place protocols** regularly.

Step 4: Prepare & Assign Responsibilities

- Assign each family member specific roles (e.g., grab go-bags, assist younger siblings, secure pets).
- Create and store **go-bags** for each member with ID, supplies, and comfort items.
- Include a **pet emergency plan** (crate, food, medications).
- Keep **important documents and medications** in a quickly accessible location.
- Identify and list **special needs** or medical conditions for each person.

Step 5: Documentation & Visibility

- Fill out and distribute a **Family Emergency Plan Document** (names, contacts, meeting points, roles).
- Place laminated copies of the plan:
    - On the fridge
    - In each go-bag
    - In glove compartments
- Ensure all children and caregivers understand and have access to the plan.

Step 6: Training & Practice

- Review the plan **biannually** and after any major changes (e.g., new job, school, or move).
- Conduct **practice drills** for evacuations and meetups.
- Teach **basic first aid, navigation, and communication skills** to all family members.
- Make it a game for younger children to **learn escape routes and safe words.**

Step 7: Include Reunification Protocols

- Know the reunification policies for your child's school or daycare.
- Make sure all emergency contacts are on school pickup forms.
- Have recent family photos and physical descriptions of each member.
- Pre-arrange a designated adult to collect children if you cannot.

CHECKLIST:
Developing a Group Security Plan for a Large Event

Attending large-scale public events can be enjoyable, but they also pose unique risks. From crowd surges to potential threats like violence or medical emergencies, it's essential to have a proactive plan for safety, communication, and reunification.

1. Pre-Event Planning (Before You Arrive)

- **Research the Event Layout:** Look at venue maps, exits, medical stations, restrooms, and entry points.
- **Assess Risk Factors:** Is the event high-profile, political, controversial, or in a crowded urban environment?
- **Assign Group Roles:**
    - Leader/Navigator
    - Safety Checker (keeps tabs on headcount, health, etc.)
    - Communications Coordinator (monitors phones, texts, radio)
- **Establish a Rally Point:** Choose a **specific, fixed location** away from the main crowd (e.g., a food truck, statue, parking lot corner, tower, or public monument).
    - Must be known **before** arriving.
    - Should be easy to describe and visible on a map.
    - Should not rely solely on landmarks that could be blocked by crowds.
- **Time-Based Fallback:** Agree on a secondary plan (e.g., "If we're separated for more than 30 minutes and can't reach each other, go to the rally point").

2. Communication Protocols

- **Designate a Primary Contact Number** for the group.
- **Use a Group Chat or Emergency App** (e.g., Signal, Life360). Set phone backgrounds to display emergency contact info on the lock screen.
- **Carry spare power:** Portable phone charger or battery pack.

- Pre-arrange **emergency signals** (text codes, phrases, or hand gestures for silent communication).

3. Identification & Essentials

- Carry a **photo ID** and a **card with emergency contacts and medical info.**
- Dress for recognition and comfort (match shirts, hats, or wristbands for children).
- Bring a basic **first-aid kit, bottled water,** and a **flashlight.**
- Have a small **notebook and pen** for writing location updates if phones fail.
- Carry a **whistle or noise device** to signal distress or get attention if needed.

4. Situational Awareness On-Site

- Identify **nearest exits and emergency shelters** upon arrival.
- Make note of **law enforcement, security personnel, and medics.**
- Avoid bottlenecks, tight spaces, or being too close to barricades.
- Keep **at least one person sober** and observant at all times.
- Watch for:
     - Sudden crowd movement or surges
     - Abandoned bags or suspicious behavior
     - Individuals exhibiting agitation or erratic behavior

5. Emergency Response Plan

- If separation occurs, **go to the rally point immediately** or within a set time.
- In case of an emergency (e.g., gunfire, explosion, stampede), **move laterally away from crowds**, not just backward.
- Use code words for **rapid coordination** (e.g., "Plan Bravo" = move to rally point quietly).
- Establish what types of situations require **evacuation** vs. sheltering in place.

6. Transportation & Exit Strategy

- Park in a **well-lit, easy-to-exit location**—reverse into the spot if possible.
- Identify **multiple routes** away from the event in case of traffic or lockdowns.
- **Carpool and consolidate vehicles** if attending in a large group.
- Leave early if crowd energy shifts or tensions rise.

7. After-Action Review

- Once safe, **check in with all group members** by phone and in person.
- Review what went well and what could be improved next time.
- Update your personal security notes and adjust future plans accordingly.

<u>CHECKLIST:</u>
Assembling Your Emergency Go-Bag

A go-bag (also called a "bug-out bag") is a pre-packed emergency kit designed to sustain you for at least 72 hours in the event you need to evacuate quickly due to a crisis such as a natural disaster, civil unrest, or other emergency.

Essentials & Documents

- Government-issued ID (photocopy + digital copy on USB)
- Emergency contact list (paper and digital)
- Cash (small denominations)
- Copies of critical documents (insurance, deed, passport, prescriptions)
- Map of the local area with evacuation routes
- A pen and a waterproof notebook

Water & Hydration

- 3 liters of water per person
- Portable water filter (e.g., LifeStraw)
- Water purification tablets
- Collapsible water bottle or canteen

Food & Nutrition

- 72-hour supply of non-perishable food (MREs, energy bars, trail mix)
- Electrolyte tablets or drink mix packets
- Utensils/spork and collapsible bowl
- Compact stove or cooking system

Tools & Survival Gear

- Fixed-blade or folding knife (quality, durable)
- Multi-tool (with pliers, screwdrivers, can opener, etc.)
- Flashlight (LED) with extra batteries or solar/crank power
- Headlamp for hands-free illumination
- Paracord (at least 25 ft)
- Duct tape (mini roll or wrapped)
- Fire starter kit (waterproof matches, ferro rod, lighter)
- Emergency whistle
- Compass (non-digital)
- Work gloves

First Aid & Medical

- Basic first aid kit (bandages, gauze, antiseptic wipes, tweezers, etc.)
- Prescription medications (3–7 day supply)
- OTC meds (pain relievers, antihistamines, anti-diarrheals)
- Tourniquet or trauma kit
- N95 masks or respirators
- Hand sanitizer and disinfecting wipes

Clothing & Protection

- Weather-appropriate clothing (layers)
- Spare underwear and hiking socks
- Lightweight rain poncho or jacket
- Hat and gloves
- Comfortable walking shoes or boots

Shelter & Comfort

- Emergency blanket (Mylar) or sleeping bag
- Compact tent, tarp, or bivy sack
- Sleeping pad
- Eye mask and earplugs (for rest in crowded places)

Communication & Power

- Pre-paid cell phone or battery backup phone
- Portable charger or solar power bank
- Charging cables
- AM/FM or NOAA weather radio (crank or solar-powered)

Sanitation & Hygiene

- Toothbrush, toothpaste, and floss
- Biodegradable soap and shampoo
- Deodorant
- Toilet paper (compressed or flat pack)
- Feminine hygiene products
- Towel and washcloth
- Ziplock bags or trash bags

Security & Self-Defense

- Self-defense tool (if a firearm then with proper permits)
- Concealment holster (if carrying a weapon)
- Flashlight with strobe mode (for disorientation or signaling)
- Extra ammunition or spare self-defense supplies

Extras (Based on Family Needs)

- Baby formula, diapers, and wipes (if applicable)
- Pet food, leash, and medical needs
- Spare glasses/contact lenses and solution
- Entertainment (deck of cards, book, etc.)

<u>CHECKLIST:</u>
Upgrading the Physical Security of a College Dorm Room

College dorms often prioritize convenience over security. While students may not be allowed to install permanent hardware, there are numerous legal, low-profile ways to improve personal safety and protect belongings in a shared or semi-public space. Check with Residence Life policies before installing anything semi-permanent.

Door Security

- **Door Wedge Alarm:** Place under the door to prevent unauthorized entry and trigger a loud alarm. (e.g., Sabre Wedge Door Stop Security Alarm)
- **Portable Door Lock:** Use a travel lock or dorm-safe secondary lock (e.g., Addalock) that doesn't require tools.
- **Door Barricade Device:** Non-permanent security braces that prevent forced entry from the outside. (e.g., MasterLock Security Door Bar)
- **Reinforce Hinges:** Ensure hinges are tight and tamper-proof (especially if the door swings outward).
- **Always Lock the Door:** Get in the habit of locking your door, even when you're inside or stepping out briefly.

Window Security

- **Install Window Locks:** Use clamp-style locks or travel locks to limit how far windows can open.
- **Add Window Security Film:** Prevent shattering with clear adhesive film (removable varieties available).
- **Hang Privacy Curtains:** Block outside view into your room—especially at night.
- **Consider a Window Sensor:** Use battery-powered alarms or sensors for extra warning against intrusion. (e.g., Sabre Window Glass Alarm)

Securing Valuables

- **Personal Safe or Lockbox:** Small but heavy or boltable safes for laptops, passports, or cash.
- **Cable Locks:** Secure laptops, monitors, and other electronics to furniture.
- **Lockable Storage Trunk:** Ideal for securing bulkier items or when leaving during breaks.
- **Document Protection:** Use fire-resistant pouches for essential papers and ID copies.

Lighting & Visibility

- **Motion-Activated Light:** Place by the door or window to alert you of unexpected movement.
- **Battery-Powered Nightlight:** Prevent tripping in a darkened room or during power outages.
- **Exterior Awareness:** Request a dorm room with visibility to exterior areas or hallway traffic if possible.

Entry Control & Room Access

- **Be Discreet with Keycards/Keys:** Don't label or leave them unattended.
- **Know Your Roommate(s):** Set clear boundaries for visitors and shared access.
- **Lock Storage Areas:** If you share a closet or drawer, secure your section individually.
- **Don't Prop Open Doors:** Common in dorms but a major security risk.

Package & Mail Safety

- **Use Secure Lockers or Central Pickup:** Avoid packages being left unattended outside your room.
- **Track Deliveries:** Get text or app alerts when a package arrives.
- **Discourage Hallway Storage:** Don't leave bikes, boxes, or valuables in shared corridors.

Awareness & Habits

- **Secure Your Room When Sleeping:** Lock the door and use a wedge or portable lock.
- **Report Suspicious Activity:** Know how to contact campus security discreetly and quickly.
- **Avoid Oversharing Location Info:** Disable geo-tags and avoid posting real-time locations online.
- **Create a "Check-In" Routine:** Let a trusted friend or family member know your schedule, especially during travel or late nights.

Smart Devices & Monitoring (If Allowed)

- **Wi-Fi Security Camera:** Pointed at the door for motion detection (check dorm policy first).
- **Smart Plug Timer:** Randomize lighting when you're away to create the illusion of occupancy.
- **Bluetooth Tracker:** Attach to valuables in case of theft (e.g., AirTag, Tile).

Final Tips

- Check with Residence Life policies before installing anything semi-permanent.
- Focus on layered security: deterrence, detection, delay, and defense.
- Ensure all upgrades are legal, non-damaging, and roommate-approved.

CHECKLIST:
Building an Emergency Medical Trauma Kit

A **trauma kit** goes well beyond basic first aid—it's designed to help manage life-threatening injuries and sustain life until professional medical help arrives. Whether for use in the home, vehicle, or as part of a go-bag, this kit should be compact, well-organized, and equipped for rapid response.

Reputable suppliers such as North American Rescue provide cost-effective, pre-built kits for almost any budget. It's essential that you *regularly train with and understand* the use case for each piece of equipment you choose to include in your kit.

Lifesaving Essentials (The "Stop the Bleed" Core)

- **Tourniquet** (CAT, SOF-T, or other proven models — *not rubber bands or flimsy imitations*)
- **Pressure dressing** (Israeli bandage, OLAES bandage)
- **Hemostatic gauze** (e.g., QuikClot, Celox) for severe bleeding
- **Compressed gauze** (for wound packing)
- **Chest seals** (vented and/or non-vented) for sucking chest wounds
- **Nasopharyngeal airway (NPA)** with water-based lubricant
- **Trauma shears** (to rapidly expose wounds)

Secondary Supplies for Stabilization

- **Medical gloves** (nitrile, latex-free)
- **CPR face shield** or mask with one-way valve
- **Emergency blanket (Mylar)** to prevent hypothermia & shock
- **Medical tape** (durable and hypoallergenic)
- **Triangular bandage** (for slings or head wraps)
- **Elastic bandages** (for joint support or securing dressings)
- **SAM splint** or similar moldable splint
- **Burn dressing** or burn gel (for thermal injuries)

Wound Cleaning & Infection Control

- **Antiseptic wipes** or iodine swabs
- **Sterile saline or eyewash** (small squeeze bottles)
- **Hydrogen peroxide or wound irrigation syringe** (optional)
- **Antibiotic ointment** (single-use packs preferred)
- **Alcohol prep pads**

Medications & Relief

- **Aspirin** (for suspected heart attack)
- **Antihistamines** (e.g., diphenhydramine for allergic reactions)
- **Anti-inflammatory pain relievers** (ibuprofen, acetaminophen)
- **Glucose gel or tablets** (for diabetic emergencies)
- **Anti-diarrheal and anti-nausea tablets**
- **Epinephrine auto-injector** (if prescribed or for severe allergy risk)

Documentation & Identification

- **Medical info card** (blood type, allergies, current medications)
- **Treatment log or notepad** (record what was done, when, and why)
- **Permanent marker** (to write tourniquet application time or ID info)
- **Copy of first aid/trauma flowchart or checklist**

Training & Readiness Add-Ons

- **First Aid & Trauma Manual** or quick-reference guide
- **Laminated instruction cards** (for TQ use, chest seals, CPR, etc.)
- **Red cross or color-coded labels** for rapid kit access
- **Blowout pouch** or separate trauma module for fast access to life-saving tools
- **Hands-on training** in TCCC, TECC, or Stop the Bleed protocols (*strongly recommended*)

Optional but Useful Additions

- **Irrigation syringe** (for cleaning wounds under pressure)
- **Finger pulse oximeter**
- **Digital thermometer**
- **Headlamp or small flashlight** (with red lens option)
- **Duct tape or medical-grade adhesive wrap**
- Zip ties (improvised restraints or gear repair)
- **AED (Automatic External Defibrillator).** These items are expensive, but in a cardiac arrest situation, combining CPR with defibrillation significantly increases survival rates from cardiac arrest compared to CPR alone, with studies showing survival rates jumping from around 7% to >30%.

Final Notes

- Check and **replace expired items** regularly.
- Store kits in **clearly labeled, accessible locations:** home, car, work, go-bag.
- Practice using every tool—**familiarity saves lives.**

CHECKLIST:
Selecting a Handgun for Home Defense

Choosing the right handgun for home defense involves more than just caliber or brand preference. It requires careful consideration of reliability, ergonomics, capacity, and your personal ability to handle the firearm effectively and safely.

*Firearms should be stored in a locked container that restricts unauthorized access - particularly from children - allowing access only to trained, responsible adults.

Functionality & Reliability

- **Proven Track Record:** Is the model known for reliability in defensive use?
- **Brand Reputation:** Is the manufacturer reputable with a history of quality?
- **Simplicity of Operation:** Can you operate it confidently under stress?
- **Tested Performance:** Has the handgun been range-tested with your chosen self-defense ammo?

Ergonomics & Fit

- **Grip Size:** Does the handgun fit your hand comfortably and securely?
- **Control Reach:** Can you easily reach and operate the magazine release, slide stop, and safety (if present)?
- **Recoil Management:** Can you manage recoil effectively for fast follow-up shots?
- **Slide Manipulation:** Are you able to rack the slide reliably?
- **Trigger Comfort:** Is the trigger pull weight, reset, and travel manageable for you?

Caliber & "Stopping Power"

- **Effective Caliber:** Is the caliber suitable for defensive use (e.g., 9mm, .40 S&W, .45 ACP)?
- **Ammo Availability:** Is the caliber readily available and affordable for training?
- **Penetration Consideration:** Have you considered the risk of over-penetration in a home setting?

Size & Capacity

- **Full-Size or Compact:** Is the size appropriate for home use rather than concealed carry?
- **Magazine Capacity:** Does it hold a sufficient number of rounds for a defensive situation?
- **Weight & Balance:** Does it feel well-balanced and stable when aiming?

Home Defense Features

- **Rail System:** Does it have an accessory rail for mounting a light or laser?
- **Night Sights:** Are the sights visible in low light or equipped with tritium?
- **Suppressor Compatibility** (optional): Do you plan to add a suppressor or compensator?
- **Manual Safety** (if applicable): Do you want a manual safety or prefer a simpler striker-fired design?

Accuracy & Shootability

- **Track Record of Accuracy:** Does the model have a reputation for practical accuracy?
- **Sight Radius:** Is the sight radius long enough to aid in precision shooting?
- **Follow-Up Shot Control:** Can you consistently keep rounds on target with rapid fire?

Maintenance & Customization

- **Ease of Field Stripping:** Can you disassemble and clean the gun easily?
- **Parts & Accessories:** Are holsters, magazines, and aftermarket parts readily available?
- **Durability:** Is the handgun built with corrosion-resistant and long-lasting materials?

Training & Familiarity

- **Consistency with Training Gun:** Does it match what you train with regularly?
- **Dry Fire Friendly:** Can you safely dry fire for practice at home?
- **Compatibility with Defensive Drills:** Is the platform suitable for your home-defense training scenarios?

Final Checks

- **Tested at the Range:** Have you fired at least 200–300 rounds through it without malfunction?
- **Trusted by Professionals:** Is it commonly used by law enforcement or security professionals?
- **Confidence Level:** Do you feel confident and competent using it in a high-stress situation?

CHECKLIST:
Selecting a Concealed Carry Holster

Choosing the right concealed carry holster is just as important as choosing the right firearm. The holster you select will directly impact your comfort, accessibility, concealment, and safety. A poor holster can lead to printing (someone being able to identify that you are carrying a gun), firearm mishandling, or even accidental discharge.

1. Safety First

- **Trigger Guard Coverage:** Does the holster fully cover and protect the trigger from any accidental engagement?
- **Reholstering Safety:** Can you reholster your firearm *without pointing it at your body* or struggling to find the opening?
- **Firearm Retention:** Does the holster retain the gun securely, even if you move, run, or bend over?
- **Passive vs. Active Retention:** Is retention adjustable, and does it fit your comfort level and needs (e.g., click retention or retention straps)?

2. Comfort & Wearability

- **Body Conformity:** Does the holster contour to your body for all-day wear?
- **Padding or Sweat Guard:** Does it have material to prevent pinching, rubbing, or sweat on the firearm?
- **Adjustable Cant and Ride Height:** Can you change the angle and depth of carry for optimal comfort and concealment?
- **Belt Compatibility:** Is it compatible with your gun belt in terms of width and stiffness?

3. Concealment

- **Minimizes Printing:** Does the holster help you conceal the firearm without the outline showing through clothing?

- **Clothing Compatibility:** Does it work with your daily attire (e.g., t-shirts, business casual, jackets)?
- **Tuckable Options:** If needed, does the holster allow you to tuck in a shirt for professional or formal settings?
- **Low Profile Design:** Is the design streamlined and free of unnecessary bulk?

4. Draw Efficiency

- **Full Firing Grip Access:** Can you get a solid grip on the firearm without adjusting after the draw?
- **Consistent Draw Angle:** Does the holster allow for a repeatable and efficient draw stroke?
- **One-Handed Reholstering:** Can you reholster safely using only one hand (no collapsing fabric)?
- **Secure Draw Resistance:** Is there just enough retention to secure the gun, but not slow your draw?

5. Holster Type & Carry Position

- **IWB (Inside the Waistband):** Ideal for deep concealment —are you comfortable with this?
- **AIWB (Appendix Inside Waistband):** Offers fast access, but requires excellent trigger protection and body comfort.
- **OWB (Outside the Waistband):** Good for range or jacket concealment—does it hug close to the body?
- **Pocket Carry:** Is the holster rigid, does it protect the trigger, and does it stay in the pocket during draw?
- **Ankle, Shoulder, or Bag Carry:** Are you trained and practiced in drawing from these less common positions?

6. Material & Build Quality

- **Durable Construction:** Is it made from Kydex, leather, hybrid, or another material built to last?
- **Sweat & Weather Resistance:** Can the holster handle moisture, heat, or extended wear?

- **Craftsmanship:** Are the edges smooth, hardware secure, and retention points reinforced?

7. Testing & Practicality

- **Fitment Check:** Was the holster molded for your exact firearm model?
- **Live Fire Practice:** Have you safely trained with the holster at the range?
- **Dry Fire Drills:** Have you tested it for drawing, reholstering, and moving around your home or property?
- **Comfort Under Movement:** Can you sit, bend, walk, and drive with the holster comfortably?

8. Legal & Situational Awareness

- **Local Laws:** Does your method of carry comply with concealed carry laws in your state?
- **Holster Accessibility in Emergencies:** Will you be able to access your firearm in the majority of daily scenarios?
- **Use With Permit/License:** Is your holster setup legal under your current carry permit or training requirements?

Tips for Choosing Among Top Brands:

- Does the brand offer **holsters for your exact firearm model**, including light/optic compatibility?
- Are there **return or fit guarantee policies** for peace of mind?
- Does the holster meet your **carry style** (IWB, AIWB, OWB, pocket)?
- Can you **test the draw and concealment** before committing to long-term carry?

<u>CHECKLIST:</u>
Selecting an SDLI Policy

Important considerations when selecting the Self Defense Liability Insurance (SDLI) policy or program that is right for *you*:

Coverage Scope

- **Criminal Defense Coverage:** Does the policy cover legal expenses
  if you're charged with a crime after a self-defense incident?
- **Civil Defense Coverage:** Are you covered in the event of a civil lawsuit?
- **Bail Bond Coverage:** Is bail bond assistance included, and up to what amount?
- **Red Flag Law Coverage:** Does the policy offer any protection or legal help if you're subject to a red flag law or risk protection order?
- **Use of Force Types:** Does coverage apply to both lethal and non-lethal force (e.g., pepper spray, tasers, fists)?
- **Home vs. Away:** Does the policy protect you both at home and in public settings?
- **Firearm & Non-Firearm Incidents:** Are non-firearm self-defense tools and empty-hand defense included?

Financial Considerations

- **Policy Limits:** What are the caps on criminal, civil, and bail coverage?
- **Attorney Fees:** Are attorney fees paid up front or reimbursed after acquittal?
- **Deductibles:** Are there any deductibles for using the policy?
- **Monthly/Annual Cost:** What is the cost, and is it reasonable for your budget?
- **Retainer Fees:** Will you need to pay out of pocket for a retainer, or is that included?

- **Lost Wages Coverage:** Are lost wages during court appearances or recovery covered?

Legal Representation

- **Attorney Choice:** Can you choose your own lawyer, or must you use one provided by the insurer?
- **Pre-Qualified Network:** Does the insurer offer a network of experienced self-defense attorneys?
- **24/7 Emergency Hotline:** Is there a hotline available to contact an attorney immediately after an incident?

Policy Terms & Conditions

- **Upfront Payment vs. Reimbursement:** Does the company pay expenses as they occur or only after legal resolution?
- **Exclusions:** What actions or circumstances are explicitly not covered (e.g., illegal weapons, intoxication, provocation)?
- **Training Requirements:** Are you required to take any classes or maintain certifications?
- **Policy Activation Delay:** Is there a waiting period before coverage becomes active?

Location & Legal Environment

- **State-Specific Laws:** Is the policy tailored to the self-defense laws in your state?
- **Travel Coverage:** Are you covered when traveling out of state or internationally?
- **Permit Requirements:** Must you have a valid concealed carry permit or similar documentation?

Additional Services & Resources

- **Education & Training:** Does the insurer provide educational materials or access to self-defense training?
- **Family Coverage:** Can you add family members to the policy?

- **Incident Response Guidance:** Are you offered guidance for what to do in the aftermath of a defensive incident?

Customer Service & Reputation

- **Customer Support:** Is the customer support knowledgeable and responsive?
- **Company Reputation:** Does the provider have a good reputation in the self-defense and firearms communities?
- **Reviews & Testimonials:** What do current and former customers say about their experience?

ABOUT THE AUTHOR

ROB CHADWICK

Photo by Keith Kamikawa

Following a distinguished 30-year career in law enforcement, Rob Chadwick was appointed Director of Education & Training for the United States Concealed Carry Association (USCCA) in 2023. In this role, he leverages decades of elite experience in tactical operations, firearms instruction, and active shooter response to lead the development and growth of the USCCA's nationwide network of over 10,000 Certified Instructors, bringing lifesaving knowledge and training to everyday Americans.

Rob retired as the head of the Tactical Training Unit at the FBI Academy in Quantico, where he served as the Principal Tactical Instructor for the Federal Bureau of Investigation. In this position, he oversaw the global readiness and tactical proficiency of FBI Agents and specialized teams. A recipient of the FBI Director's Medal of Excellence for Training, Rob represented the United States as the keynote speaker at the 2017 International Symposium on Active Shooter Response in Prague.

Throughout his career, Rob has held multiple advanced certifications, including Senior Instructor status in Tactical Operations, Firearms, and Emergency Vehicle Operations. He has served as an FBI SWAT Team member, sniper team leader, and a nationally certified Emergency Medical Technician. His extensive protective service includes assignments on the security details of six United States Attorneys General, most recently serving as an Agent-in-Charge for Attorney General William P. Barr.

Before joining the FBI, Rob began his law enforcement journey in the Special Operations Division of the Fairfax County Police Department in Virginia. His lifetime of service and training excellence now informs his mission to empower citizens with the knowledge and skills to protect themselves and their loved ones.

www.ingramcontent.com/pod-product-compliance
Lightning Source LLC
Chambersburg PA
CBHW051152120626
46547CB00012B/1047